NEMIAH

THE UNCONQUERED COUNTRY

NEMIAH

THE UNCONQUERED COUNTRY

TERRY GLAVIN

AND THE PEOPLE
OF NEMIAH VALLEY

PHOTOGRAPHS BY
GARY FIEGEHEN,
RICK BLACKLAWS
& VANCE HANNA

New Star Books
Vancouver
1992

Published by New Star Books in association with the Western Canada Wilderness
Committee.

New Star Books Ltd.   Western Canada Wilderness Committee
2504 York Avenue   20 Water Street
Vancouver, B.C.   Vancouver, B.C.
V6K 1E3   V6B 1A4

Publication of this book is made possible by grants from the Canada Council and the
Cultural Services Branch, Province of British Columbia.

Design: Barbara Hodgson
Map by Gaye Hammond
Special characters created by Stuart Morris
Production: Audrey McClellan
Printed and bound in Canada by Kromar Printing Ltd., Winnipeg
Printed on recycled, pH-neutral paper
1 2 3 4 5   96 95 94 93 92

Canadian Cataloguing in Publication Data
Glavin, Terry, 1955-
   Nemiah: the unconquered country

   Includes bibliographical references
   ISBN 0-921586-22-1

   1. Chilcotin Indians. 2. Chilcotin Indians — Legends. 3. Indians of North America —
British Columbia — Nemaia Creek Valley. 4. Indians of North America — Nemaia
Creek Valley — Legends. 5. Nemaia Creek Valley (B.C.). 6. Legends — British
Columbia — Nemiah Creek Valley. I. Title.
E99.T78G43 1992 971.1'75 C92-091697-X

CONTENTS

FOREWORD

The wind ripped manuscript pages from pickup truck dashboards and flung them out windows. People wanted to be sure we had it all just right, so the book went from place to place. Everything took a long time. There were a lot of meetings. It was a lot of hard work.

The result is this book, and it came about because of the goodwill, cooperation and sacrifice of a great number of people, from Nemiah and from outside, from Chilcotin and beyond, by nenqayni and midugh.

It's been like that ever since the logging started moving in. Patrick Lulua saw it coming. Cindy English pioneered the research. Annie Williams kept a firm grip on the reins, and everybody got to work. There was Inez Setah, Orrie Charlieboy, Edmond Lulua II and Carey Billy. There was Adam William, Illa Setah, Hank Setah and Margaret Lulua. From their work, the Nemiah Declaration was prepared.

People wanted to tell the world who they really were, too. So a book committee was formed: Annie Williams, Alan Haig-Brown and Paul George. Leona William and June William talked to the old people. I got picked to pull it together, and settled in for the autumn months of 1990. Gilbert Solomon left his mistletoe job over in Alexis Creek and joined up. Gilbert's dad, Henry, and all the Solomons were always there to help. Dave Dinwoodie pitched in where he could and Walter Lulua watched out for us. All along, Rick Blacklaws, Gary Fiegehen and Vance Hanna stayed long-time friends of the Chilcotin country. Their loyalty to this project helped keep the whole thing alive.

For much of the written record of the events of the last century, I leaned heavily on the tremendous scholarly contributions of Edward Sleigh Hewlett and Robert Brockstedt Lane.

Most of the Chilcotin stories that appear in verbatim form throughout this book are making published appearances in the English language for the first time. The storytellers were William Setah, Rosalie Johnny, Eugene William, Eileen William, Henry Solomon, Danny Sammy and Francis Sammy. Their narrations were gathered, recorded, translated and related by Annie Setah, Gilbert Solomon, Roger William, Hank Setah and Margaret Lulua.

The job of looking things over and fixing things up fell to Ubill Lulua, Gilbert Solomon, Gene Cooper, Joyce Cooper, Simon Setah, Bobby William, Francis Setah, Benny William, Roger William, Marty Solomon, Annie William, Walter Lulua, Bernie Solomon, Blaine William, William Setah, Henry Solomon, Iver Myers, Dennis Lulua, Agnes William, Eileen William, Juliana Lulua, Madeline Setah and Margaret Lulua. Among others.

Throughout this book, the reader will note unusual orthography in Chilcotin words (with thanks to Stuart Morris for creating the special characters for New Star). Something that looks like a question mark, the occasional 's' with a hat on it, an 'i' with a line through it. That sort of thing.

To an outsider's ear, the Chilcotin language is a strange and beautiful thing, and the orthography has been developed by linguists to ensure that pronunciations remain correct. It is not as intimidating as you might think.

Some words are easy — Sit′ax sounds something sort of like see toch, with the 'ch' sounding the way Scots pronounce those two letters together. (An 'i' with a line crossed through it denotes the short 'i' sound, as in 'hit.') Lhasasʔin actually sounds vaguely similar to the usual spelling, Klatsassine. The 'h' and the 'l' are pronounced together, at the roof of the mouth, behind the teeth, until you get Lhas-awss-een. That question mark without the dot is a glottal stop. A glottal stop means you stop the breath from coming out of your mouth and start again, so: Lhas-awss-(stop)-een. An apostrophe in the middle of a word does a similar sort of thing: it puts some kick in the syllable that follows.

Midugh is easy. It means white man, and it's pronounced mee-dough. Tŝ′ilʔos is much like it looks — something like Tzill-(stop)-awce. The hat on the 's' modifies the sound of the vowels that follow it in that word, giving

them a softer, more open sound: 'o' becomes 'aw', etc. If the s-with-a-hat *follows* a vowel, then that preceding vowel takes the softer sound. Thus ʔesdluŝ sounds like (stop)-esdlowce, and ʔEŝch′ed is pronounced something like (stop)-us-ch'ed, with the last syllable getting that little extra kick.

Then there's xajaghindilh. You're on your own.

TG
August 31, 1992

THE NEMIAH DECLARATION

Let it be known as of August 23, 1989:

We, the Tsilhqot'in People of Xeni, known as the Nemiah Valley Indian Band, declare that the lands shown on the map attached, which form part of our traditional territory, are, and shall henceforth be known as:

Nemiah Aboriginal Wilderness Preserve

Let it be known that within the Nemiah Aboriginal Wilderness Preserve:

1. There shall be no commercial logging. Only local cutting of trees for our own needs, i.e. firewood, housing, fencing, native uses, etc.
2. There shall be no mining or mining explorations.
3. There shall be no commercial road building.
4. All-terrain vehicles and skidoos shall only be permitted for trapping purposes.
5. There shall be no flooding or dam construction on Chilko, Taseko, and Tatlayoko Lakes.
6. This is the spiritual and economic homeland of our people. We will continue in perpetuity: a) to have and exercise our traditional rights of hunting, fishing, trapping, gathering, and natural resources; b) to carry on our traditional ranching way of life; c) to practise our traditional native medicine, religion, sacred, and spiritual ways.
7. That we are prepared to SHARE our Nemiah Aboriginal Wilderness Preserve with non-natives in the following ways: a) with our permission

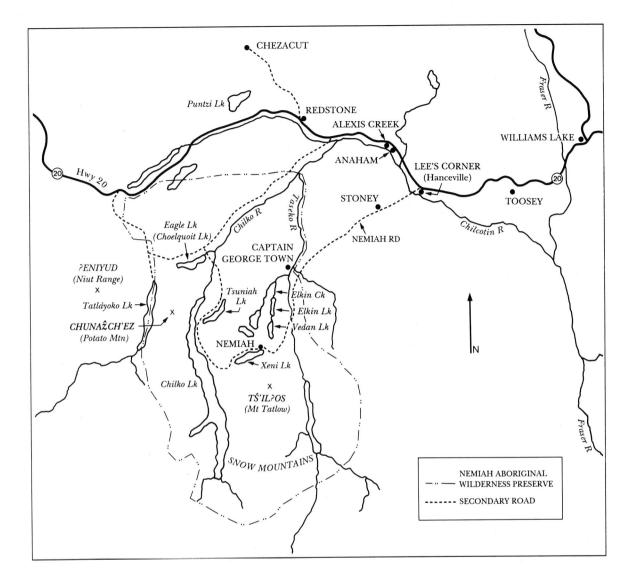

visitors may come and view and photograph our beautiful land; b) we will issue permits, subject to our conservation rules, for hunting and fishing within our Preserve; c) the respectful use of our Preserve by canoeists, hikers, light campers, and other visitors is encouraged, subject to our system of permits.

8. We are prepared to enforce and defend our Aboriginal rights in any way we are able.

You build a big campfire.
Maybe tomorrow you're going to go,
so you start singing.
Maybe you got a drum.
Something like that.

So you start singing.
You just dance around the campfire,
these guys going to war
on some other people,
some other place. So
you just dance,
and the next day comes.

And you've got to go where you're going
to war.
You don't know if you're going to
come back. You don't know if somebody's
going to kill you.
That's how he goes.
Like that.

Henry Solomon

CHAPTER 1

CAPTAIN GEORGE TOWN

Walter Lulua doesn't worry much about things.

Like a lot of the Xeni gwet'in, as the Chilcotins in the mountains around the Nemiah Valley know themselves, Walter lets Tŝ'ilʔos do the worrying. He prefers to count on Tŝ'ilʔos to watch over the people. To take care of them.

So Walter wasn't really worried about old Eugene William, but it seemed to make sense to go out and see how he was getting along and hear what he had to say for himself these days. Besides, Eugene told stories. He could tell a good story about Tŝ'ilʔos, who had turned into a mountain a long time ago, around the beginning of the world. And Walter figured I'd like to hear some of Eugene's stories for myself.

Tŝ'ilʔos used to be a man. According to the Government of the Province of British Columbia and the maps it issues of the Chilcotin country, Tŝ'ilʔos is Mount Tatlow, 10,058 feet high, about 60 miles in a straight line south-southwest of Alexis Creek, and about an equal distance north-northwest of Pemberton. Tŝ'ilʔos is more or less in the middle of a big blank space on the map. On one side of the emptiness is the blue line the Fraser River draws up through the centre of the province, and on the other side, the narrow inlets that carve into the Coast Mountains.

At first, the snow-covered peak of Tŝ'ilʔos seems to hover in the clouds, floating above the green and rolling pine forests that blanket the Chilcotin plateau as you approach from the northeast. Which is the only way to approach, at least by road (unless you know how to connect a series of wagon

NEXT PAGE:

Tŝ'ilʔos, seen from the road into the Nemiah Valley

trails through the bush to the northwest, in which case you can make it that way, with luck and with good weather). The only real road into the Nemiah Valley, the heart of Xeni gwet'in territory below Tŝ'ilʔos, is from the northeast, from Stoney. Gilbert Solomon once told me that if the weather was right, and you were standing in the right place, you could see the top of Tŝ'ilʔos from as far away as Riske Creek, even though it is a mountain among mountains. Like nearby Taseko Mountain, 10,047 feet. Chilko Mountain, 8,871 feet. Or any number of mountains in the volcanic outburst of the Chilcotin Range, which rises up against the Coast Range and boasts B.C.'s highest peak, Mount Waddington (13,104 feet), and mountains like ʔEniyud, who used to be a woman when Tŝ'ilʔos was still a man.

What started Walter thinking about old Eugene William was that he didn't show up for his ride into Williams Lake for that return visit with the doctor.

A few weeks back, on the first leg of a long trip down into Kamloops to see a doctor about a hearing aid, Eugene said he didn't feel quite right. In the old days, when someone in the Nemiah country got sick, there were old medicine people to turn to for help. These days, when someone in the Nemiah gets trouble enough to think about seeing a medical doctor, they find their way into Williams Lake by way of the road, which connects the Nemiah Valley to the village of Stoney and the short haul across the Chilcotin River to pavement at Lee's Corner. From there, you head east and out the Chilcotin Highway, across the Sheep Creek bridge and into town. But Kamloops was the closest place with an ear doctor. So that's where they were headed when Eugene started feeling sick, around Riske Creek.

Walter said he'd never known Eugene to feel faint like that. Eugene was in his early seventies. He was born in the bush and didn't speak much English. He liked to live the old way and didn't make a fuss about things, so Walter figured it must be pretty bad for Eugene to complain. They stopped at Williams Lake, and the doctor there said Eugene's problem was his heart. It was bound to give out on him if Eugene didn't quit working. So Walter made another appointment for Eugene, for a thorough medical once-over and the tests the doctor wanted.

When the day came for Walter to pick him up at the band office down in the Nemiah Valley, Eugene didn't show.

THE HORSE'S SPIRIT

As told by Francis Sammy

A while back, our grandmother Annie William, Francis's mother, told him about the time when they were going to go up Mount Tatlow to pick beartooth and dry meat. This is around July and August. There was three families going up Mount Tatlow with pack horses and saddle horses. Grandmother had to leave one horse behind because he was sick. He was a really good horse. So they left one person there to watch the horse and Francis said he couldn't remember the person's name. Anyway, Grandma and the other families headed up the mountains. They got quite aways near Tatlow when all of a sudden the horse that was sick caught up with them and he was just running. Some of them were trying to stop this horse but couldn't. Anyway, this horse ran ahead of them towards the beartooth picking. They tried to catch up to the horse but couldn't. The next day the person that was watching the horse caught up with them and told them the horse died. So that horse that ran by them was his spirit. It must have wanted to go up the mountain. The horse died somewhere in Danny William's field.

So Walter had been a little bit concerned about how Eugene was doing, all the way out there at the end of a wagon trail that leads out of a corner of the Nemiah Valley. But he knew better than to worry too much. Walter knew there were all kinds of things to worry about if he put his mind to it.

Walter's wife, Annie, was the chief of the Nemiah Valley Indian band, as the Xeni gwet'in are known in English. He got all the worry he needed first hand because these times were some of the roughest since the times after the Chilcotin War almost 130 years earlier, when the surviving warriors fled deep into these mountains and stayed hidden out and more or less forgotten to the outside world until the Canadian military engineers, on a federal Indian Affairs contract, finished the road through to the Nemiah Valley in 1973.

What was rough about these times was that all over the Chilcotin country, the government had just about handed over the forests to companies like Carrier Lumber, P & T Mills, Fletcher Challenge, Lignum, Weldwood, West Fraser and Jacobsen Brothers. They were taking an allowable annual cut that had grown rapidly from 2.5 million cubic meters in the regional supply in 1980 to 4 million cubic meters by 1985. Another million cubic meters' worth was being taken out of the bush each year from private lands in a regulation-loophole scam the government was always vowing to fix but never did. There was even a government plan in the works to permit the cutting of an extra 265,000 cubic meters for pulpwood every year for 25 years from stands the forest ministry had originally set aside for preservation. At the height of the logging season, 250 fully loaded logging trucks passed by Lee's Corner on the way out of the Chilcotin every day, and if the government had its way, timber from the Xeni gwet'in country would eventually supply sections of the convoy. Annie and the band council had already geared up to fight the company's logging plans with a court case based on Aboriginal trapping rights, and the band had teamed up with the Western Canada Wilderness Committee behind something they decided to call the Nemiah Declaration, sort of a declaration of co-dependence based on Aboriginal rights and sustainable development. The idea was that if the Chilcotin Indians had to make their last stand, they'd do it in the Xeni gwet'in country, where they made it in 1864.

But for now, at least, things hadn't changed that much. Even after the military engineers pushed the road through from Stoney, there was a lot that hadn't changed. The Xeni gwet'in remained largely forgotten by the outside world, and those things that had changed were okay by most accounts. The road meant no more six-day journeys by saddle horse and wagon to Lee's Corner and back, for one thing. It meant an easier trip out to the rodeos at Chezacut or Riske Creek, so that there were calf-roping contests and wild cow riding and lahal games only a day or two from home. It meant Chilcotins with black bullrider cowboy hats and names like Hank and Otis and Ubill and Agat were starting to show up in the stores in Williams Lake every other Friday or so. People weren't perfectly clear about just where these particular Chilcotins had come from, and they didn't have much money to spend and they didn't speak English much, but they sure seemed a happy bunch.

Life was still pretty well the same as it had been when Walter was a boy back in the 1960s, growing up on moosemeat and wild potatoes with his brothers and sisters out in the mountains. The road didn't bring in much traffic from the outside, except for the occasional hunter or fisherman, and the descendants of the fugitive warriors of 1864 still made their way through the forests in the shadow of Tŝ'ilʔos in horse-drawn wagons, speaking their own language, drying fish gaffed at Henry's Crossing and harvesting bear-tooth up in the alpine. Walter and Annie were determined to see that things were left as they were in the Nemiah Valley and everybody else intended the same, no matter what the logging companies had to say. As far as anyone could tell that's the way Tŝ'ilʔos felt about it, too.

Where Walter and I were headed that particular day to see if we could find Eugene William was nowhere near the road that appears on the map. Although the place we set out for that morning is known to the locals as Captain George Town, there's no such place on any map. It's a cabin or two and some fenced pasture of swamp hay and one or two hay cribs tucked away in a series of low meadows in a far-away valley. There's certainly no town there at all, and by all accounts there never was.

It tends to be like that all over the Chilcotin country. Maps aren't of much use. Nothing written in English is of much use in finding your way around.

For one thing, it is Indian country, and the Indian villages rarely show up on any maps, even though that's where most of the people in the Chilcotin

Carrier Lumber's sawmill
in Anahim Lake

A clearcut in the Chilcotin

country live, because most of them are Indians. And when a reserve does show up on a map, it's just as likely to make things more confusing.

There's Anahim Lake, an Ulkatcho Carrier village on the far western edge of Chilcotin country where hardly any Chilcotins live now, and clear across the Chilcotin near the eastern frontier is Anaham village, where the chief of the same name settled with his community back in the late 1800s. But Anaham (spelled 'am' rather than 'im') shows up on the map as Alexis Creek, which is the nearby white village. There is an Alexis Creek band, but they live way out at Redstone, about 25 miles west of Alexis Creek. Redstone should not be confused with another Chilcotin reserve known officially as Stone, but which everybody in the Chilcotin knows as Stoney.

And the Eagle Lake the Nemiah people talk about is the lake on the map that shows as Choelquoit Lake, not the Eagle Lake that appears up by Tatla quite a few miles to the north. And the Nemiah Valley, the Xeni gwet'in heartland, usually shows up as Nemaiah Valley (spelled with the extra 'a'), a dot on the map at a place called Konni Lake, which is really an attempt at spelling the way white people pronounce Xeni Lake. The Nemiah Valley was named after the first chief of the Xeni gwet'in known to the outside world, ten chiefs ago. The second chief known to the outside world was Chief ʔAchig, who is said to have bitten the ear off a settler named Elkins, after whom Elkin Lake is named. Chief ʔAchig had a son who somehow ended up with the name Captain George, and that's where Captain George Town got its name.

And there's no 'village' as such to be found at that dot on the map that shows as the misspelled Nemaiah Valley beside so-called Konni Lake. There is an old log church at one end of the lake, a few miles later there's Dixie's general store and a few miles further there's the band office that was built after the first one over at Lhizbay burned down a few years ago. Then there's the school, but if the school was on the map it would be wrong, too, because it somehow got the name Naghataneqed, which is the name of the beach on the opposite side of Xeni Lake a few miles back, where the log church is. There are some standard-issue reserve houses here and there, but the Xeni gwet'in never paid much attention to the meagre reserves the government drew on maps back in 1916. For the most part the 250-odd members of the Nemiah Valley Indian band live spread out, in the old Chilcotin way, over a

CHIEF ʔACHIG

As told by Henry Solomon

Henry said a long time ago there was a white guy named Elkins. Henry said he didn't know his real full name. Elkins was trying to move into Nemiah. Anyway, he had his camp set up over Lhizbay Lake, just five miles east of Chilko Lake, and a Nemiah chief by the name of ʔAchig told him that the boundary is the mountains that surround the country, and told him, you can move anywhere, but not in this valley. ʔAchig told Elkins he'll give him a week's time to move out of the valley, or I'll move you out myself.

So ʔAchig left Elkins and went home. A week later ʔAchig came back to see if Elkins obeyed his command. When he got there at Lhizbay he found out Elkins hadn't moved.

So ʔAchig went over to Elkins' camp and told him, I gave you one week to move out, and if you didn't I'd do it myself, now since you didn't obey my orders I'm going to move you out myself. Elkins wasn't scared of ʔAchig. He figured ʔAchig was just another Indian trying to push him around, and that the Indians didn't own any land as far as he was concerned, so he figured he can just move in.

So ʔAchig and Elkins started to fight. They fought for quite a while. Elkins is supposed to be a tough person, Henry was saying. Anyway, ʔAchig finally started to tire Elkins out, then he got a good hold of him and bit his ear, and ripped a big chunk off, then Elkins gave up and found out Chief ʔAchig was serious and that he was telling the truth about the land.

hundred square miles or so from one end of the Nemiah Valley near Anvil Mountain, to the other end down on the shores of Chilko Lake. And that's just where they live when they're in their houses, which seemed to be a pretty rare occurrence. Mostly they're just out there, fishing at some river, making the rounds from a trapline cabin, hunting in some valley or tending their small herds of bush cattle on some far meadow in the thousands of square miles of rugged mountain country they've called home since who knows when.

Which is out where Eugene William was, somewhere deep in a narrow valley another three hours of white-knuckle 4x4 bullriding deeper into the bush over a boulder-pocked track from Xeni Lake. It was autumn, and the aspen and cottonwood were turning gold and copper in the long, warm afternoons.

"Pull over here, if you like," Walter said. By my guess we were about half way through the narrow valley of pine and poplar forests on the way there. At least I guessed we were, since we'd put Vedan and Elkin Lake behind us about an hour earlier and we were now in a country of serpentine creeks, beaver ponds and the occasional coarse-running stream. Walter stepped out of the truck. "I'll show you a good place to gaff spring salmon."

Walter Lulua knows about these things. He grew up in these mountains. Killed his first deer with a .22 when he was seven years old. His mother taught him how to shoot. Nellie Lulua was a grand woman who raised six kids, mostly on her own, and raised cattle on the side, which she had to herd into Lee's Corner on her own when the road was no more than a horse trail. Walter slept on a bed of groundhog furs and liked life just fine until the priests managed to find him and brought him in to the dreaded Saint Joseph's Mission in Williams Lake. Those were the days when escape was particularly hard because the only way back to the Chilcotin country was over the Sheep Creek bridge and the priests used to maintain occasional checkpoints there to catch homeward bound Chilcotin runaways. After Walter's fourth summer back home, Nellie agreed never to send him back again. Ever since, it's these mountains that Walter's come to know better than anything else.

We staggered the first few steps down towards an oxbow the narrow and wandering river had pushed through the lush, high grass. Good place to cast a dry fly, too, and I had my flyrod in the back of my pickup.

Tŝ'il?os (Mt. Tatlow)

Chilko Lake

Tŝ'ilʔos

Spawning sockeye
(ts'eman, in Chilcotin)

Then we smelled it: a long-dead, half-eaten spring salmon in the sun-parched grass. And then another. Then another.

Those big springs make their way all the way back up here to spawn. From the mid-Pacific, up the Fraser River to the mouth of the Chilcotin River just below Williams Lake. Up the Chilcotin River to the bend where the Chilko River comes in just east of Redstone. Up the Chilko to the Taseko River and up the Taseko to the stream that appears on those maps as Elkin Creek. All headed for the rocky streambeds in these hills where they were born.

Walter pushed back the brim of his black cowboy hat and looked around. He took another few steps, stopped, and pushed a clump of the tall grass aside with his cowboy boot. Another dead spring salmon.

"Bear, looks like," he said.

A loud *crack!* echoed from across the narrow oxbow bend. An even louder tearing noise followed it. One of the treetops was moving. The dead tree was bashing its way through the trees to the ground, but its fall was broken in the upper limbs of the thicket. At the base of its trunk, the berry bushes shuddered and shook.

"Maybe grizzly bear, looks like," Walter said calmly. He smiled. Maybe. Maybe not.

We took our time getting back to the truck ("You always walk slow away from grizzly bears," Walter said), climbed in, and slowly bashed our way over the wagon track through the pines towards wherever it was Walter expected to find Eugene, who had made the trip a week or two earlier at the reins of his wagon, which, in these mountains, is considered the sensible mode of transport for such journeys in and out of cattle camp. My pickup moved like an old man on all fours, but soon the valley began to open up in meadows and grass-thick sidehills and finally it bloomed into the copper bright fields of Captain George Town, where Elkin Creek meanders through low willows on its way north to the Taseko.

From the edge of a swampy pasture, we made our way on foot towards a cabin on the far side of the meadow, on a low rise above the creek where a log had been hauled for a footbridge to the other side. Walter made the 30-foot crossing with ease. I was halfway across when I made the mistake of looking down.

William Setah's outfit

In the shallow river below, schools of rainbow trout swam by. Tiny ones, nice ones, a huge one. Another big rainbow. Schools of tiny whitefish, or maybe squawfish. Juvenile springs. That was when I remembered my flyrod in the back of my pickup, back there somewhere. I turned to see how far back it was. It was the last thing I saw before I lost my balance, except maybe Walter standing there with his hands on his hips as he said, "Hold it."

So I was soaking wet for the last short walk into Captain George Town. Mabel William sat outside the old cabin on a woodblock, laughing, nodding her head towards my soaked jeans and boots and talking with Walter in Chilcotin.

"He's out back," Walter said.

Which is where at long last we found Eugene. He was smiling and sitting straight-backed atop an ancient iron-and-leather haymower with two chestnut plough horses harnessed to it.

His face beamed with a wide grin from under the peak of an old baseball cap and he looked happy and stout and sunburned and a lot younger than his 73 years.

Eugene and Walter exchanged hellos and laughed together and talked a while in Chilcotin. They discussed the haymower, built by "Frost and Wood, Smith's Falls, Canada." It was getting a bit primitive 100 years ago, but it was the type Eugene learned how to use when he was ten years old, and since it works fine, it's fine by him. Eugene laughed some more. His first words to me, which Walter translated from the Chilcotin, were: " The grasshoppers are the best."

Eugene was in the best of health as it turned out, and what he had to say about grasshoppers turned out to be sound advice. Not that I had asked for advice, but it must have looked like I needed some.

Eugene just sat there on the back of his haymower, smiling. The plough horses were fitted out with blinkers and oatbags, lazy and content, and Eugene wasn't going anywhere either, so Walter stopped worrying about him and we joined Eugene's four-year-old grandson, Benson, scrambling around the scrubby grass catching grasshoppers. Benson, whose real name is Brent but whose nickname comes by way of Eugene, was better at it than we were. In a couple of minutes we had enough to fill my shirtpockets, so we headed back to the pickup for my flyrod and an extra steelhead rod for Walter, and within a few minutes of shinnying back across the log and scrambling through scrub willows littered with bear-caught spring carcasses, Walter and I had landed and released five rainbows apiece.

Eugene William was right about grasshoppers, and the general feeling is that he's right about most everything he has to say, but the thing is he doesn't say much. It had been a long day for him already, and he was tired, so Walter and I spent the afternoon fishing.

As it turned out, it had been a long day for a lot of people in the Nemiah. The word was that Carrier Lumber, one of the timber companies that had been granted permission by the provincial government to clearcut the forests in the Xeni gwet'in territory, was busy building a road that day into the northwestern corner of the Nemiah band's trapline, near Henry's Crossing. The word spread fast, and everybody was getting anxious. Back down in the Nemiah Valley, Benny William and Marvin Baptiste, both former chiefs assigned to keep an eye on the loggers, were talking about what to do about Carrier's road. They were making plans to hire a small plane to fly over the area to see what was going on.

The next time I made it out to Captain George Town it seemed to make sense to stay on a little while to help Eugene and his family put in the swamp hay to carry his 40 head the rest of the way to calving time. I figured he could probably use the help, as long as I didn't get in the way, and Walter had told me that Eugene had some thoughts on all this talk about the logging companies moving in on the east and the north, and he also had some story about the Chilcotin War that I should probably hear. By the time I got back out to Captain George Town, Benny and Marvin had hired a plane to see what Carrier was up to, and what they found was that the company's roadbuilders had pushed through a 100-foot-wide strip that clipped off a half-mile piece of the corner of the trapline. In its own small way, that was history. It was the first time the Xeni gwet'in territory had been touched by the forest industry, and when people around the Nemiah Valley looked for precedents, the subject of the Chilcotin War kept coming up.

TATLOW

As told by Eugene William

Long ago a guy named Roy Haines was riding the country to see if he could raise cattle out here. This was when people around here didn't own any cattle or very many horses. They just moved around. Them days there was no moose at all and very few deers, just fishes is mostly what they lived on and also berries, wild potato and bearteeth plant. Things like that.

Anyway, this guy Roy Haines rode this country and he figured this was a hell of a place to raise his cattle because he seen all the grass around stood tall and on the hillsides was at least a foot tall and down low was two feet or more. I guess Sammy William was riding with him and he told Roy the story about Mount Tatlow. He told Roy that this peak called Mount Tatlow was once a man before. Tatlow had a wife named ʔEniyud. Between them they had six kids altogether. I guess they split up. Couldn't get along with each other. Each of them took three kids and separated. Tatlow turned into a rock with his kids above Xeni Lake and ʔEniyud turned into a rock with her kids over the other side of Tatlayoko Lake. Sammy told Roy that when you point at Tatlow he'll make it rain or snow on you. Anyway, Roy told Sammy he was going to bring his cattle and horses out here because he figured there's lots of hay out here. So Sammy told him that Tatlow didn't like white men.

Roy Haines and his cowboys brought some of his cattle out anyway, then they went back to pick up the rest of the cattle and started to chase them out towards Nemiah. When they got close to Nemiah, where they could stay for awhile, he

Tŝ'ilʔos, looking southeast from Nemiah

got his men to ride ahead to check the other cattle in the valley. When the boys got close enough to see the valley from the hill, they found out that it snowed in the mountains. So they went to check it out. When they got down in the valley they found that all the snow on the mountain slid down about four feet high in the valley. So their cattle were stranded in the slide, plus the horses they left there.

Then the boys went back to Roy Haines and told him, so Roy took his cattle back and made a ranch over by Chilko River, other side of Stone, which is now called Chilko Ranch.

What had also happened was Eugene had killed a white-tailed deer with the .22 he keeps in brackets fashioned from upturned deer hooves among the kerosene lamps, cowboy hats, cups and saucers, coats and saws that hang from the walls of the tiny cabin where he lives with Mabel and little Benson and whoever else happens to be passing through. Another thing was that Eugene's dog, King, had a limp from getting his paw caught in something while he was chasing jackrabbits across the pasture, but it didn't seem to bother him much and he kept going after jackrabbits. And Adam and Blaine and Willard, nephews to Eugene in one way or another, had come up to help put the hay in, and so had Dave Dinwoodie, a Mexican-born, Alberta-raised Montana resident from the University of Chicago who had arrived in the Nemiah Valley a couple of weeks earlier with a vague plan of staying on for as long as it took to learn how to speak Chilcotin. So lots had been going on, and it seemed like the important thing at the moment was to sit for a while and drink ledi, as Chilcotins around here call tea, and talk about the affairs of the world. And about how long it would take to get the hay in and how many haystacks these meadows might make.

There's more than 200 acres of swamp hay here. Much of it is thick with tangled willows or poplar or aspen, despite the best efforts of the beavers, which have cut timber from the sidehills and dragged it to the creek. They've cleared broad trails through the bush and built their lodges at every bend and oxbow, and there's clearly more beaver here than there ever were people. And this was swamp hay, not that 'tame hay' they make down around Stoney that you can cut three times in a good year, and so the discussion went until Eugene stood up and said, "Well, you going to help me with that deer?"

So we headed off into the bush behind the cabin, with little Benson scurrying along behind. We carried the deer back from the trees where Eugene had gutted it the night before after hauling it down from the hills. We carried it past the square pole-corral of an old fish-drying rack down to a grove of small pines in the afternoon sunlight. The wind was warm and blowing strong from the south, and clouds unravelled across the sky. Mabel gathered pine poles for the drying rack, and Eugene went off to cut some young birch for more poles. He came back with enough to lash together a tripod with crosspoles balanced

THE GIRL THAT TURNED INTO A ROCK

As told by Rosalie Johnny

My grandmother showed me how. That is how I know about this.

The first time when a girl menstruates, they don't drink from a cup. That's if people had any cups in those days. They used to drink from tin cans in those days. When the girls menstruated, they used to be shy about it. Girls that were menstruating didn't stay in the villages. They used to live in the bushes. This menstruation period lasted three days or more.

Once this girl went down to the river to get water. She filled the palm of her hand with water to drink. In those days, that was all that was allowed.

A young man followed the girl down to the river to try and rape her but the girl didn't want to look at him because she wasn't supposed to during her menstruation period. He met her on the way down to the river but she crouched down and that's when she turned into a rock, in that position. This is how the girl turned into a rock, long ago. Maybe this girl was from around here (not particularly Nemiah Valley) but it was so long ago that it's hard to really say for sure.

The next time a girl menstruates, so that she won't get sores or get sick, she should take a piece of white cloth and go to this rock (the one that the girl turned into) and stuff it in the crevice of the rock and say, "Grandmother, help me not to get sick anymore." That's what you say.

from it to the limbs of a small pine tree on the other end, and Mabel went to work on the deer. Benson did his best to help.

Mabel knelt and went to work on the hind legs, slowly and carefully cutting the hide away from the flesh, working her way up to the belly and along the sides. She lay the deer on its back and deftly skinned another hind leg, pulling the hide from the fat and the meat, like pulling sleeves from a child's arm. In her red kerchief, blue cardigan and tartan dress, Mabel hurried without effort. While her quick fingers worked their way along the belly she talked gently to Benson in Chilcotin, telling him how to hold the animal for her in the way that would make her work go easy. Eugene knelt beside her and cut sections of meat from the animal, passing each to me and pointing to the pole on the drying rack it should hang from. Willard and Blaine gathered firewood and built a slow blaze beneath the rack to keep the flies away.

Within an hour, Eugene was sharpening a stake at both ends to roast the animal's ribs over the fire, and we all sat around in the afternoon sun and the sweet smell of poplar smoke and venison. The ribs roasted in the flames and the smoke drifted across the meadows.

Mabel and Eugene sat together and talked and laughed quietly, the two of them being married now more than 50 years. They married in Redstone, her village, during priest time, one of the two or three times a year one of the Oblates from Saint Joseph's Mission made the week-long trek out to the far Chilcotin. It was the same day Pilip Pateece married a girl from Anaham and his old friend Ubill married Oolia Charlieboy, but they're all dead now and only Eugene and Mabel are left.

They have a dozen children of their own, enough grandchildren that they've just about lost count, and they live the old way with about 40 head of cattle, here or in the far meadow about seven miles further in, and down in Nemiah where they winter. Since they're getting on in years, their sons, maybe Benny or Boysie, bring them fish, and so does Benson's dad, Edmund Lulua, who's sometimes called 'Edmund Two' because there are two Edmund Luluas in the Nemiah. Sometimes he's just called Eetman after the fashion of Chilcotinizing outside names.

Eugene was born up the Taseko River, on the trapline, in a tent in the dead of winter. He and Mabel raised their own family out towards Tatlayoko in the northwest corner of the territory, where Carrier Lumber was hoping to start clearcutting pretty soon, but over the years he's spent more time down towards Xeni Lake where the swamp hay is richer and there's more of it. He's run his cattle here at Captain George Town and the Nemiah Valley for a dozen years or so, and before that it was in the Eagle Lake country for about fifteen years after moving south from the Tatlayoko.

Eugene sat quietly, whittling on a stick, fidgeting a little in his old workboots. He brushed his hands on his jeans and pulled his baseball cap low over his eyes in the piercing afternoon sun.

"Well, we say we don't want them to get all the logs," he said about the logging companies' plans. "Sometimes, we need it sometime. All of this would be open, no tree pretty soon. Game, he won't stay in the open like that, you know? Just like killing all the game. That's what we say.

"Game, I guess he got to have some timber, to lay down under the tree when the snow comes, rain. The log company, he cut all the tree, all the way."

He looks worried when he talks about it.

"I don't know what we would do with no timber. There'd be no more game, too. I don't know what we're going to eat."

So what do you do?

"Try to stop them. I don't know. We'll think of something, I guess," he says. And then something about it makes him laugh.

"I guess government, they don't want to stop it, but we'll just try, anyway," he said, and he smiled that broad smile of his, and his thoughts took him elsewhere.

"We got lots of time, eh? That's the reason, out here, living out here like this, it's kind of quiet. Now we go to town, and we want to come back in, eh?"

Eugene's been as far as Vancouver four times in his life, and it's about as far and as often as he cares to go. He says he doesn't like it there because there are too many people, too many buildings. The last time he was there was the time 30 Xeni gwet'in headed out in two vans and five pickup trucks on the thirteen-hour trip to Vancouver to formally submit their court case against the logging companies. That was December 14, 1989, and there were even more buildings then than the time he went before.

Like Eugene says, it's kind of quiet out here. The years carry in to one

del way of
life

another with the seasons. People move with their animals from one meadow to the next, sell some calves and sometimes an older one to bring in some money, decide which heifers to keep and which of the fatter cows to hold back for milk in the springtime, and life moves slowly. With the dying day there wasn't much point in getting much work in, so back in the cabin after a meal of venison and rice and carrots and potatoes, Mabel and Eugene chatted away, with Mabel looking out through the cabin window as the last light of day fell over the fields.

Adam was asking when Captain George, son of the second Nemiah chief known to the outside world, was here last.

"It's over forty years, anyway," Eugene said, in English. "He's buried at Nemiah."

Eugene and Adam talked a bit in Chilcotin, and laughed. People seem to end up laughing whenever Captain George's name comes up.

This was his place at one time, and the cabin was here before Benny was born, Eugene said. That was more than forty years ago now, so there's no telling when it was built, but the story is that Captain George himself built it.

The sun went down over the mountainside and the horses grazed down by the shallows. Little Benson was looking at the pictures of Mabel's three-year-old copy of *Crochet World* magazine in one hand and a half-eaten deer rib in the other. He was the first to fall asleep.

The coyotes were the last.

They kept each other awake half the night howling to each other from the pine forests on one side of the meadows to the hills across the valley, and the owls took up their work in the frosty air before daybreak. By morning, southbound flocks of Canada geese were adding their voices high above Captain George Town, and we sat down to a breakfast of Mabel's deer steak and eggs and coffee.

The first job of the day was to harness the two work horses to the rough-hewn haysled Eugene had cut from the pines and lead them across the deep creek with the haysled in tow. Eugene and Willard hitched the sled to the horses, pulled them around and headed them towards the creek to cross them at the shallows, with King following along.

"Did you see that dog running through the field?" Willard asked on his way across with Eugene. "Jumps right up in the air, like that," he said, throwing his hand above his head in sharp strokes, "just like a deer. Chasing something." The limp wasn't bothering him anymore, and the dog disappeared through the willows down to the south. In the distance, Tŝ'ilʔos rose in the morning mist with what we were certain was a fresh fall of snow on his peak.

With an uproar of hooves, the haysled splashed into the creek with Eugene at the reins. The pine pole uprights shuddered and heaved with the force of the tow, straining the baling wire Eugene had used to lash the whole thing together. King appeared out of nowhere and swam along behind, and the whole works floated downstream intact behind the snorting work horses until Eugene guided them back up the bank and through the willows. He brought them to a dead stop and stood there proud and smiling, reins in hand. He caught his breath and said, "Sometimes I use a wagon, but with a wagon you got to take everything off before you stack."

Which is why he prefers the ʔesdluŝ, which is the Chilcotin word for haysled.

"Sled's better than wagon," Blaine explained. "Wagon gets stuck, and it's too bumpy."

The haysled is only slightly less elaborate than Eugene's Frost and Wood horse-drawn haymower, and only slightly more sophisticated than his horse-drawn hayrake — 24 half-circle rake teeth hung from an adjustable bar beneath a cast-iron seat, the whole business suspended between two iron wagon wheels and pulled by two pine poles harnessed to two work horses. That's the extent of Eugene's heavy machinery, and he's proud of his machines, but later on, as he laboured with the haysled chains, his breathing was heavy.

"Just doesn't want to quit," Adam said. "He's a working man. He just can't sit around."

Mabel walked out to the hill behind the cabin to cut some more deer meat from the drying rack, and the rest of us headed out for the day's pitchfork work on the meadow. Adam's GMC Sierra pickup was put into service to haul

ʔEniyud (Niut Range)

DREAMING ABOUT EAGLES

As told by Danny Sammy

Sammy dreamt about two eagles fighting one time. One was a golden eagle, the other one a bald eagle. I guess Sammy was dreaming he was laying in a big opening on this side of Xexti Lake. He was watching these two eagles going at each other high above him and all of a sudden they attacked each other and both fell in the tall spruce trees. Then he woke up and told the story because he figured that the dream would give the power of the golden eagle. They say when your power is a golden eagle you would have to do whatever the golden eagle wants you to do or it will kill you if you don't obey your powers.

Danny William with
his nephew, Adam William

Haying at
William Setah's ranch

the sled, and that allowed Eugene to take it slow for awhile. We worked through the morning and the sun burned away the frost, and with only a few traces of cloud in the sky it's hot again soon enough and the grasshoppers are back. We managed about a dozen haystacks in each sledload, hauling the load back to the crib, where a 60-foot-high tripod rig lifts cables from underneath the haysled load in a kind of sling that pops up with a hard tug from the bumper of Adam's pickup. With each load pulled up and over into the crib, Benson jumped and tumbled around and tried to pretend, at least, that he was serious about keeping out of everybody's way.

After a lunch of deer stew, potatoes, carrots, rice, bannock, jam, cookies and coffee we were back at it, and by late afternoon Benson was no longer alone in the growing haystack in Eugene's corral-sized crib. A convoy of pickups carrying Nemiah families from down the valley came to visit with Eugene to see how he was getting along, and Benson's leaps into the hay were followed by the somersaults of Erikk Lulua, Brenda Lulua, Celia Setah, Joline Marie William, Charlene William, Yolanda William, Geraldine William, Wesley William, Lois William and Linda Setah. Eugene sat at the end of the day whittling wood shavings in front of an open fire outside his cabin. Mabel was cooking deer stew in a big pot, trying her best to keep us all fed.

Eugene was rested and happy. He was getting his hay in and he had visits from his relations in the bargain, and he liked to hear them speaking Chilcotin still, even if some of them did have a hard time of it since they spent so much time speaking English. Little Benson was that way. He was four years old, but he could understand Chilcotin, even if he couldn't speak it all too well.

"I know a little bit about chinook," Eugene said, in the slow and deliberate way he speaks. Chinook was the trading jargon used to speak to outsiders before the people learned English.

"My dad, he told me a little bit. I had a little book. Chinook words, with English. I lost it, though."

He looked across the field at the gang of Nemiah kids jumping from his haycrib fence into the haystack.

"Kids play with it. All wore out," he said, thinking again about that book.

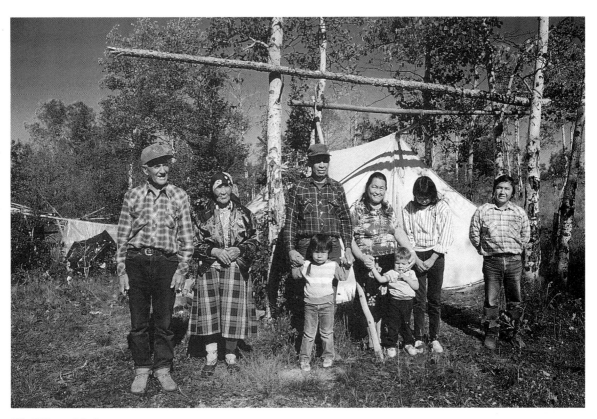

The Ekks and Lulua
families in camp

He smiled and went on that it would be nice if he still had the book around to show people, at least.

"Anyway, I'm 73. Going to be 74 in November. I should be in good shape right now, but I got a sickness, you know. Diabetes. High blood pressure."

That was what the doctor had told him the day Walter took him into Williams Lake. The doctor told him about how those things can wear on a man's heart, and that's why he wanted to see Eugene again.

"Last time, doctor give me a pill. Say I pretty near had a heart attack. Doctor tell me, no work. Take it easy. Take it easy for five, six weeks. That was about five weeks ago now. But I can't just do that. I gotta work."

He smiled again.

"But I take my time," he said.

One of those broad smiles came over Eugene's face again, and he laughed. He sat forward on the woodblock in front of the fire and looked out across the fields, deep into the trees on the far side of the winding creek where Walter and I used his grasshoppers to catch trout a few days earlier.

Eugene talked about what had brought him to these hills apart from the hay for his cattle. "Moose, deer, coyote, fox, lynx, marten . . . no. No marten. Mink. Some mink down here. Weasel. Wolverine . . . not many wolverine. Sometimes you see them, eh?"

I asked him about the logging companies again, and what people were going to do. These very hills showed up on government forest service maps in Alexis Creek as timber available for P & T Mills. The government said it was all theirs as soon as they decided the best way to get across the Taseko River.

And then Eugene said, simply, "Samandlin."

This would be the Chilcotin War story Walter told me Eugene had.

"Old people have story about that one," Eugene said. "Samandlin, he come up, I guess, Eagle Lake. He went all down that way east, I guess."

He sat comfortably on his woodblock and whittled away with his old hunting knife.

"They say, them old days, 'If he win at Eagle Lake, he win everything,' eh? He's going to get it all. Everything, I guess.

"But he lost. He gets killed."

California bighorn sheep

(Samandlin is the name that Chilcotin people, for their own reasons, have given to Donald McLean, a retired Hudson's Bay Company trader who was hired by colonial authorities to help command a group of white volunteers in an expeditionary force against the Chilcotin warriors of 1864. It may be that the name Samandlin evolved from a Chilcotin pronunciation of the French 'monsieur' — some Chilcotins developed a familiarity with French from the days of the fur trade — coupled with an abbreviated pronunciation of McLean. Whatever the case, his killing was a crucial event in the incidents of 1864, and from the Xeni gwet'in point of view, Samandlin's death was the decisive encounter in the struggle for the defence of their homelands.

The Chilcotin War, as it's come to be known, was the only instance of significant military resistance to colonial authority waged by Aboriginal people west of the Rocky Mountains.

Apart from Métis resistance at the Red River, the Northwest Rebellion of 1885 and occasional skirmishing across the Canadian west, British and Canadian sovereignty was asserted west of the Great Lakes without much sustained bloodshed. But in the Chilcotin country, by the end of 1864, nineteen white men and four Indians were dead, and six more Chilcotins were to die on the gallows.

Most British Columbians are unlikely to have even heard of the Chilcotin War. And the popular accounts of it, such as they are, tend to present a story about a gang of bloodthirsty if tragic Indian characters engaged in a losing battle against the unstoppable march of civilization. But when all the 19th-century folktales are put aside, what clearly emerges is that the Chilcotins involved in the resistance clearly meant to wage war against hostile and unwanted intrusions from outside, and they more or less won, or at least fought the thing to a draw.

It was the construction of a wagon road from the coast that provoked the initial and most bloody encounter in the war. The road was a grand scheme hatched by a big-business speculator named Alfred Waddington. He proposed to move miners from the coast to the Cariboo goldfields in a relatively quick and inexpensive fashion, sort of a Coquihalla Highway of its day. In the Office of Lands and Works in the 1860s, no more regard was given to Aboriginal title than in the Ministry of Forests in the 1980s. The attack on the road crew in the Homathko Canyon went unquestionably in favour of the Chilcotins: fourteen roadbuilders killed; no Indian casualties. The ensuing encounters also went generally in favour of the Indians, and the road, which Waddington planned to put straight through the heart of the Xeni gwet'in territories, never did get built. And no road had made its way through the Xeni gwet'in country until the Canadian military engineers pushed their road through unmolested in 1973.

The war "ended," by most accounts, after five warriors turned themselves in and were hanged at Quesnellesmouth, with the sixth dying at the end of a rope behind the old New Westminster jailhouse.

The official version of the story never held much water. Even a substantial body of white opinion at the time saw the hangings as a cowardly and deceitful response to peace talks the warriors appear to have proposed prior to their capture. To this day the Chilcotins are inclined to say they won, if the war really ended at all, and questions remain about who died on the gallows. After the main fighting was over most of the warriors fled into the mountains with their families, anyway, and they were never captured.

What is clear is that the heroic figure that shows up in popular accounts as Donald McLean had it coming to him when a bullet ended his life on a hill a few miles from Captain George Town, in the bush up by Eagle Lake.

Eugene whittled some more, smiled, and began his story.

"One of the Chilcotin, I guess, they went up around Eagle Lake, around there. Nemiah. Kind of a dokdox, like, you know, his own way. A dokdox."

"Samandlin?" I asked. "A dokdox?"

"No," Eugene answered. "Chilcotin himself. A dokdox."

"So what's a dokdox, in midugh?" I asked, midugh being the word for white man, or the word for the white man's language.

"Just something . . . like, you know what they call it. You know when somebody's coming. You find out right away, even you don't see him."

"Oh," I said, thinking this should have been clear to me a little quicker. 'Indian doctor' is to Chilcotins what 'witch doctor' might be to a Catholic priest. Chilcotins sometimes take an English word with a roughly equivalent meaning to a word of their own, put a Chilcotin spin on it and hand it back again.

"You mean, like a doctor."

THE BLIND MEDICINE MAN

As told by Eugene William

A long time ago, the natives used to have stronger powers than natives today. The natives a long time ago didn't have guns so they used bows and arrows. The medicine men back then used to shoot arrows very accurate and it was more dangerous than guns. There was this one blind medicine man who used to hunt with a bow and arrow. The medicine man's wife used to spot the animal and tell him where the animal is located so the blind medicine man can aim in that direction. His powers told him where exactly his prey was so he could shoot it. He never failed.

Sandhill cranes

Eugene: "Yeah. Like a dokdox."

"Like an Indian doctor."

Eugene: "Like what we call Indian dokdox."

"So. A dokdox."

Eugene: "Yeah."

At that point I remember thinking that by now, Eugene must be reckoning that I'm a little slow. But he was kind enough to be patient and he continued on.

"So, Samandlin, he come over there, Eagle Lake. He went out on a trail. That's an Indian trail, huh? Indian had no horses, just walking, up in that mountain. He dig the wild potato up there, I guess.

"So they went down to check the trail, eh? Two guys went down there, to check everything. Then pretty soon, Samandlin. He's coming up that trail. He don't know that trail, but he's coming up that trail."

The brief encounter McLean was about to have with the Chilcotin people on that trail near Eagle Lake was not his first.

His relations with them went back twenty years, to the time he spent as a trader at Fort Chilcotin, a Hudson's Bay Company outpost on the Chilcotin River that operated intermittently between 1829 and 1844.

Most of their neighbours embraced the Hudson's Bay trade but the Chilcotins displayed little interest in selling furs to the HBC, and company officials were often vexed by what they described as the "audacity," "insolence" and "menaces" of the Chilcotins, who also show up in HBC records as "troublesome and disorderly." McLean didn't exactly contribute to improved relations, and it was under his tenure at Fort Chilcotin that the outpost was shut down and removed to Kluskus, in Carrier country.

McLean shows up as a "devoted family man" with a "reputation for fairness" in a popular account of the events of 1864, aptly titled *The Chilcotin War*, written by Kamloops journalist Mel Rothenburger, himself a descendant of McLean. McLean also shows up in a book of reminiscences written by the Protestant missionary R.C. Lundin Brown, entitled *Klatsassan*, after the reputed leader of the Chilcotin warriors. Brown describes McLean as a man who was "immensely popular for his kindliness, his unwearying energy, and the good will with which he undertook any work that wanted doing." This is the same man to which even the Reverend Brown attributes the deaths of as many as nineteen Indians prior to the outbreak of hostilities in the Chilcotin country, the same man who distinguished himself in the winter of 1849 by murdering an unarmed elderly Indian in a Carrier village near Quesnel because the old man didn't know where a murder suspect was hiding. During the course of that same "investigation," McLean's party shot and killed another unarmed man, fired a musket point blank into the head of an infant, and shot the dead child's mother in the shoulder.

McLean was cleared by HBC officials as having behaved with 'entire satisfaction' in the Quesnel murders, just as he has been rehabilitated by popular white history and the official story of the Chilcotin War.

It certainly wasn't McLean's kindliness that prompted colonial governor Frederick Seymour to hire him out of retirement at his ranch down at Hat Creek for the mercenary work that needed doing in Chilcotin country. And McLean was anxious to get on with his work. He put on his trademark bullet-proof metal vest, quickly raised two dozen of his own volunteers to head off into the Chilcotin, and was out scouting for the enemy on his own the day he died, defying explicit orders from expedition leader and colonial commissioner William Cox to stay back in camp with the others.

"He find the trail all right, that Samandlin," says Eugene.

"Then somebody, he take out his knife out of its sheath, and cut from kind of a tree, right down on the trail. Leave 'em on a trail."

That was the trap.

At this point, Eugene takes a firm hold of his knife, holds his thumb against the dull edge of the blade to steady his hand, and cuts a thin slice from the stick he's whittling. He takes the strip he's cut and puts it on the ground in front of him.

"He put it on the trail," he says, pointing with his knife to the strip of wood on the ground between his feet.

"He leave it on the trail. That one, like this," he says.

Again, Eugene takes a firm grip of the short pole in his left hand, and pulls the blade of his hunting knife towards him with his right hand, peeling off a strip of wood and dropping it to the ground. He looks at the two shavings between his boots, then looks up, and starts whittling some more.

"So Samandlin come there, and he's a long time on the trail, I guess."

Eugene sits upright on his woodblock and looks down on the ground in front of him.

"He wanted to find out how long ago that one there. So he put it in his mouth."

Eugene picks up the shaving and puts it in his mouth.

"I guess, green tree, I guess. He want to find out. Maybe it's dry, maybe it's wet yet."

Samandlin takes the bait. A Chilcotin marksman takes aim.

Eugene's quiet for a moment.

"Pretty soon, somebody . . . bang. Over there."

Eugene points towards the trees out behind the cabin.

"Well, that first one, I guess he miss. Two guys. So the second one, he shot him, Samandlin."

"Two guys," I repeated. "Second one shot him."

"Yeah," Eugene said.

"I guess he's going up a hill, eh? Kind of warm, eh? Kind of hot. So he took off his shirt, like that. Somebody heard they got steel shirts. I don't know what kind of shirt that is."

"I heard about that," I said. "I heard about it."

"So that time, he's not wearing his shirt, I guess. Bullet, he can't go in that shirt. It just fall down, I guess. But it was opened up. Right here."

Eugene points to his chest.

"Right here. That's where the Indian hit him, with a bullet. That's why he killed him."

Eugene slowly whittles a few more shavings from the sharpening end of the stick in his left hand.

Who killed him? I asked.

"Sachayel."

Mabel was standing by the fire. Eugene asked her the same question, in Chilcotin. She had been listening a while, turning some bannock on the iron griddle.

They talked back and forth in Chilcotin, then Eugene said, again, "Sachayel."

Tŝ'il?os

He thought for a moment, and then he said: "Two guys, I know. I don't know which one."

Rothenburger names the marksman as somebody named Anukatlk, a scout that joined the warriors late in the war. The Reverend Brown says it was someone named Shililika.

Mabel was standing quietly at the iron griddle over the open fire. She glanced over and said to Eugene, "Hatish."

"Hatish?" asked Eugene.

"Hatish," Mabel answered.

"Hatish. Yeah," Eugene said. He nodded in agreement, but he looked uncertain.

"He was the other guy?" I asked.

"Yeah."

"Sachayel," I said, "but maybe Sachayel, maybe?"

"Yeah," Eugene said. "Maybe that one. I don't know. Don't know for sure."

So maybe Sachayel, maybe Hatish, and then there are the names Anukatlk and Shililika, and I'm reminded about the clouded identity of the very leader of the Chilcotins who was hanged at Quesnel with the others. In the official court records he's identified as Klatsassin, sometimes known as Klatsassan, sometimes Klatsassine, and sometimes Klatassin. In Chilcotin, it's Lhasasʔin, and Adam William explained to me one day that translated into the English it means "We don't know who it is."

It's not clear who might legitimately claim credit for shooting Samandlin, but like Eugene said, the idea was that if he won at Eagle Lake, he'd win everything, that he'd get it all. But he lost. He got killed.

And Commissioner William Cox's expeditionary force of 50 men turned around and headed back on a quick march to Puntzi Lake, leaving Samandlin's body buried somewhere in the bush.

"Who was the dokdox? What was his name?"

"Oh, some kind of a dokdox. You know, just a dokdox."

"But we don't know his name?"

"No."

"But the people here knew he was coming, because the dokdox told them?"

"Yeah. Pretty near all of them were like that, I guess. Somebody coming, they find out. Maybe he feel them, I guess. That's the way with dokdox. If somebody's coming, they feel kind of funny, I guess. That's how they know somebody's coming."

There's not too many people around that are like that anymore, he said.

"Them old people, though, that's what I mean. Indian dokdox. You know, when you get sick, he'll fix you up. That's why they call them dokdox.

"Same kind they got in Williams Lake," he said, like the doctor he was supposed to see that day he didn't show when Walter was waiting for him at the band office down in Nemiah Valley.

"Only different way."

FRANCIS AND AGATHA SETAH

In this house there is a portrait of the Virgin Mary, there are palm crosses and crucifixes and a clothesline in the living room above the woodstove. On a peg on the wall hangs the jaunty brown cowboy hat that Francis Setah, 63, likes to wear with the bright kerchiefs he's known for.

Francis Setah sits on a couch. He is wearing a blue T-shirt and bluejeans and his hair, greying on top, is tied back in a short ponytail.

He sits back and smiles and talks about his younger days, sleeping on moosehide and mountain goat blankets in the old cabin that still stands just a short walk from this house. Francis lived with his grandmother in the old house. He cut firewood in the snow, barefoot, in the days when there was nothing but a saddle horse trail through here. She taught him how to shoot squirrels to eat and how to skin the tiny pelts to sell for a quarter each, and he remembers being poor, but he doesn't have a good recollection of the stories she told him about Old Setah, or Sit'ax, who would be, as close as we could reckon, Francis Setah's great-uncle.

He was really too young to be able to remember those stories. Johnny Setah's mother, who was Old Setah's wife, had a lot of stories about him, too. But she took them to the grave with her, Francis says.

But, Francis says, he remembers this much: "If they found midugh, they'd kill them. They'd kill them and take their belongings."

Midugh means white man.

He speaks to Gilbert in Chilcotin, and Gilbert nods and turns to me.

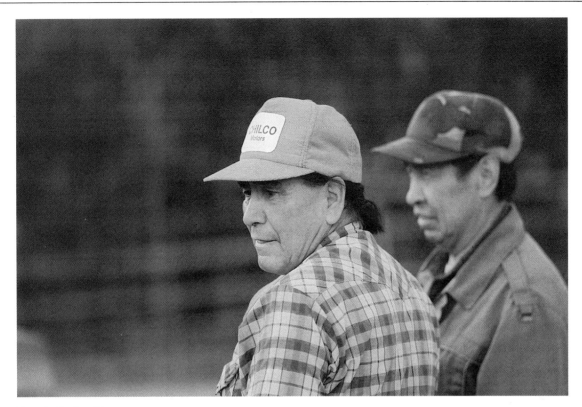

Francis Setah, with

Ubill Lulua

"Otherwise there would have been lots of midugh," Gilbert says. "Too many midugh."

Then Francis speaks again in Chilcotin, and Gilbert nods, and turns to me again, and smiles.

"His grandmother's dad missed Samandlin."

I ask Francis through Gilbert who his grandmother's dad was.

Francis replies: "ʔEzulhtsin."

It's a name I haven't heard, one not accounted for by Eugene William, and one I haven't come across anywhere. Unless it's the same person as Nezulhtsin, one of the old-timer people that Eagle Lake Henry found living in an underground house and suffering from the sickness that raged through the Chilcotin in 1918. Gilbert says he's not sure.

It's that thing with names again.

It takes Francis a few moments to tell Gilbert the story, and as he talks he speaks with his hands as much as his voice.

Gilbert was brief.

"They were coming down the mountains, to get some supplies, and they noticed horses, "ʔEzulhtsin and the other guys. They were making something, filing something, putting shavings on the ground."

This is the story Eugene told me.

"The others were scouting there. That's where they shot them."

And then a word that's particularly hard for me to pronounce. Gilbert and I talk it over and it would seem like it's the word for flintlock. Or muzzle-loader. It means 'rock-in-its-mouth.'

There was another point Francis wanted to make, and he spoke in Chilcotin, then in English. He had said earlier that it was a saddle horse trail through here when he was growing up, but they couldn't afford saddles.

"You wanna go someplace, you take a pack horse. No bridle. You just tie a rope around his nose and hit the trail."

And that was about it for the warrior who missed Samandlin and his muzzle-loader. As for the old days when Francis was a boy, it was 50 cents for a carton of .22 shells and six dollars for a single-shot .22 rifle.

Francis Setah's wife, Agatha, sits at the other end of the couch in a pretty pattern dress, busily sewing deerhide gloves by the light of a propane lamp. She reminds him, speaking softly in Chilcotin, that there were good things about those days too, like the rabbit-skin blankets the women would weave for their babies, how nice and warm they were. She makes her point delicately and returns to her gloves, the kind of gloves she used to sell in the old days at the Williams Lake stampede, the kind that earned her that prize in 1985 at the Williams Lake native friendship society's crafts competition. Beautiful beaded gloves that rank alongside her beadwork jewellery.

There's a point in that, Francis nods, smiling, and a pack horse with a rope around its nose could get you clear across the Snow Mountains and down into Lillooet to trade buckskin for dried apples or dried berries with the ʔEŝch'ed people down there.

Agatha is known, as Chilcotin women with that name are known, as Agat. Agat is a Stoney Chilcotin. She's one day older than Francis, and she has been his wife since 1947 when the priest married them after midnight mass at the tiny Church of Saint John the Baptist in Stoney. She smiled as her quick fingers pushed the threaded needle in and out of the supple deerhide and talked awhile about drying berries with bush grass.

Francis is a Nemiah Chilcotin, a Xeni gwet'in, and he was born on Potato Mountain, "under a tree, I guess."

"Yep. That's right. Can't go to hospital then. No hospital then, eh?"

No hospital, and no school, and Francis was spared Saint Joseph's Mission. There was no road in or out of Nemiah. Just that saddle horse trail, all the way to Lee's Corner. A three-day ride. Maybe for Christmas, and for supplies in the springtime.

"Three days to go that way, three days to come back. Or you can go by canoe, go across in a canoe across Chilko Lake."

Or the old-style home-made rafts, he remembers. You could get around well enough on them, lashed together with moosehide and your gear battened down and your horses swimming alongside.

That's how Francis got around when he was growing up, "living out," as they like to say, with his father Little George Setah, his stepmother Louise, his brother Willie, sister Margaret and half-brother Vincent. They spent their winters out on their trapline, living in tents, hunting and fishing and digging beartooth and wild potato from springtime to the autumn and back to the trapline again.

"Everybody was healthy and busy," says Francis. "Every day, things to do."

Saddle horse, canoe, log raft, sleigh in winter and horse-drawn wagon when the ruts weren't too deep. And then the first pickup truck, which Francis reckons must have been the one-ton Sammy Bulyan bought, the one he used to park on the far bank of the Taseko back around 1950, before the road was put through on this side of the river.

That one-ton would have been the first, unless you count the two nuns from Anaham who came down in a four-wheel-drive jeep to pick up Gilbert's aunt, Teresa Isnardy, who was pregnant and past her time and a cause for concern in the valley. That was a cold, cold winter and the nuns drove their jeep right across Xeni Lake, packed up Teresa and headed out the same day.

That was about the same time as the first bridge crossed the Taseko, but it was rickety and jerrybuilt and there wasn't much of a road to hook up with on the Nemiah side of the river anyway. It went in at about the same time as what Francis calls the 'first house,' the first building in the Nemiah country that was any more than the usual rough-hewn log affair. The Indian agent came in and had some 'houses' built but the only benefit Francis remembers was the new ones didn't drip mud in heavy rains like the old ones with their sod roofs, so they were a sight better in that respect at least.

"I still got my wagon," Francis says with pride. "In 1934 I got it, and I still got it. It's got the same tires on there. Wooden spokes."

As for children, Francis and Agat had none of their own, although they did raise Lorna Myers, but she's a grown woman now and she's long since moved off.

First trip to Williams Lake: Francis remembers it was some time in the 1940s, He was 14 or 15 when he got a job in haying time, 50 cents a day at a ranch down by Chimney Creek.

"Chimney Creek. Or maybe it was Four-Mile Creek. I worked for three weeks, then. I made more than ten bucks, eh? I bought myself a cowboy hat. It was two bucks, two something. Right now, I don't know what they cost, new. Maybe seventy bucks, I think."

Francis still hasn't made it to Vancouver.

As for cattle, Francis and Agat acquired their first cow in 1955. Agat won it in a lahal game. Back then there were few Nemiah families who had ever owned cattle. There was Captain George's family and Johnny Setah's family and Sam Bulyan's family and a handful more, but that was about it. Nowadays, Francis and Agat have about 47 head.

Wild potato (sunt'iny,
in Chilcotin)

CHAPTER 2

OLD-TIMER PEOPLE

In the days before the road came through, Henry Solomon had been regarded as something of a dokdox, like the kind Eugene had talked about. He'd married Eugene's sister, also named Mabel, and although at 60 he was a lot younger than Eugene, Henry still knew medicines and could help look after sick people, and he had ready answers for most questions people might ask. I'd met him at his cabin the previous winter, and back then Henry had sat by his woodstove and said there were some new questions people were asking, questions he didn't have answers to. Like what might happen to the moose if the logging companies came through.

Still, Henry had answers to a lot of questions even yet, and Eugene and Walter and the others thought he would know some things that might make some sense of what was going on. So we went looking for Henry down at his home place out by Lhizbay, but we'd just missed him. He'd hitched up his horses to his wagon and was headed out some back route on his way up the Taseko River where his herd was ranged.

We found Henry after two days of waiting for him to show up on the road somewhere. He was sitting on a stump beside his campfire in a grove of copper birch by the old log church down at the head of Xeni Lake. There were no big questions on Henry's mind that afternoon. He was watching the campfire and drinking a cup of coffee while Mabel cleared knots from the trout net stretched on the grass in front of her. Their horses were tethered

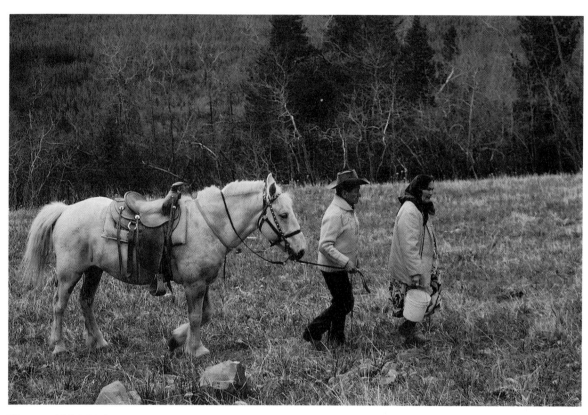

*Henry and Mabel Solomon
going to pick wild potato*

down by the beach and their dogs, Insko and Lhin, were sleeping under the Solomons' laden wagon.

Two cowboys appeared at the head of a wisp of dust down the road from the south. They'd come from the old Perjue ranch and they'd been along here earlier looking for a heifer.

"Cowboy looking for sek'i," Henry said lazily, using the Chilcotin word for cow. "Ahmullicanside cowboy," meaning American cowboys. Kelly Rudd and his brother-in-law Tony are from Idaho, but they're Canadian now, or as Henry said, "Ahmullicanside xajaghindilh," meaning they came here from the States.

Henry stood up, tucked his hands in his pockets and walked towards the road and asked Kelly, who runs the cattle operation for the Perjues, if he'd seen anything.

"Nope," Kelly called back. "There's nothing down there, Henry."

Tony, who helps with the cattle when he's not riding trail for the Elkin Creek ranch, concurred.

"Nothing," he said.

Henry smiled and said: "Should have roped him around the head."

Kelly agreed. He was aiming for the head but the rope tangled in the heifer's hooves and she broke free, but there was no use talking about it now. The two cowboys tied up their horses and joined us by the fire. Henry told them to pour themselves some coffee from the pot, and the three of them talked about the big kokanee somebody pulled from the lake a while back and all the dolly varden out there. Not too much kokanee, Henry pointed out. Mostly dek'any and sabay. Rainbows and dolly varden.

Kelly suggested to Henry that his father's haybales were selling cheap if Henry ended up short and needed some for his winter feed, and Mabel smiled, gathered her net from the grass and stood up. She doesn't speak much English and she didn't seem much interested in cowboy small talk anyway. She carefully returned her net to its burlap sack and walked down to the beach in the dying sunlight.

The talk turned to the logging, and the agreement was that nobody's at all impressed by what's been going on. Kelly talked about the time he used to work as a faller, and he said he was glad he'd put it behind him. There were

Madeline Setah drying fish

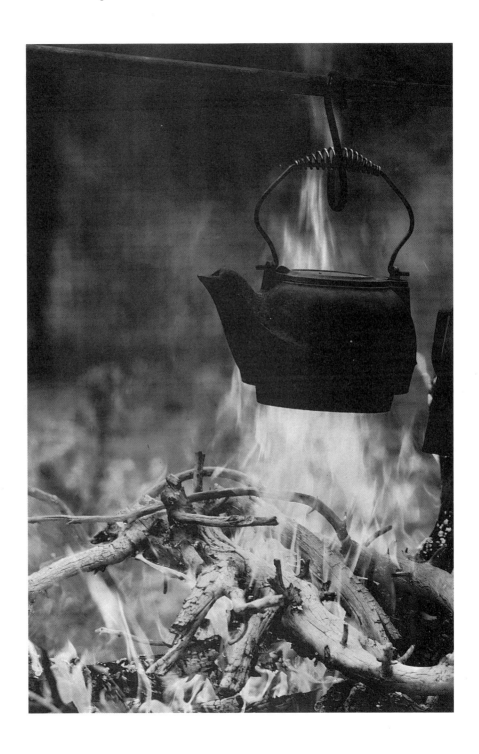

GAMBLING AT MOUNTAIN HOUSE
As told by Francis Sammy

Long time ago at Mountain House, he was saying, they used to gamble there and get together. One time they said they heard a trumpet outside the house and every one of them got scared of the sound because it was very clear and loud. Setah then went outside to see what was the sound, where it was coming from. He found out what it was. (Setah was a very strong medicine man. His power is the beaver.) It was an angel standing out there. The angel told him, you people shouldn't gamble and you guys are too noisy. The angel said he lived not very far from the cabin, near a lake. Then Setah chased him away. Since then no one has ever gambled there again. In fact, no one gathers there anymore.

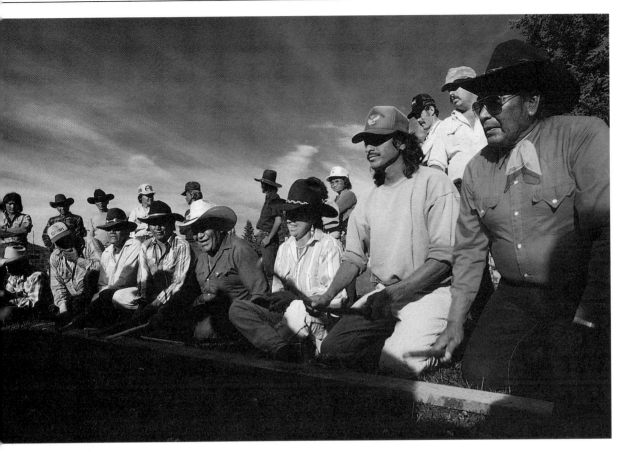

Playing lahal

THE ANGEL RETURNS TO
MOUNTAIN HOUSE
As told by Francis Sammy

One time a kid named Baptiste Dester long time ago seen a person with some pack horses and a saddle horse going by or through Mountain House cabin. I guess Baptiste seen him going through on the other side of the barn (don't know if the barn is still there) so he ran over there to get a closer look. When he got there Baptiste said it felt like someone slapped him in the face really hard, but there was no one there. Anyway, this guy who was riding a horse and leading pack horses, Baptiste said he had a long tail. When he got slapped, or when he felt he did, he got scared and started screaming and running towards the house. When he got in he dove under the bed. His parents got worried so they got Setah to sing with Baptiste. Setah sang with him. Setah said he was the angel that was leading the pack horses. He said the angel was whipping Baptiste with a willow or a prickly bush in the back.

Setah said he must be punishing Baptiste for doing bad things. Anyway, Setah chased the angel away and he never bothered Baptiste again. So that's twice Setah met with the angel at Mountain House, so he must stay near the lake around Mountain House.

modernize

three men cutting ten loads a day when he started down by Big Creek, and now there's one man in a machine cutting twelve loads every day, and there's new logging shows all over and he couldn't see how a thing like that could last.

"I figure if they get over the Davidson Bridge at all, then they've got their foot in the door," Kelly said, referring to the span the military built across the Taseko in 1969 for the road it was building from Stoney. "A lot of people are concerned about the logging. I mean, look at the way they're doing it nowadays."

They way they were doing it nowadays throughout the Chilcotin plateau was to more or less ignore what the local people had to say and let the forest companies have what they want. And they were moving a little closer to the Xeni gwet'in country each year, using feller-buncher machines that could cut, limb and stack a pine in a matter of minutes. They were moving west through the bush like lawnmowers.

Nobody in the Chilcotin knew quite what to do about it.

For starters, the Chilcotin country is one of the last areas of North America where cowboys and Indians still form a majority, and neither half of the community was much inclined to pay too close attention to the affairs of the world beyond the hills around them. So when it started happening, nobody really noticed.

When the changes came they were gradual, and they were mostly confined to Williams Lake, anyway, like when the Williams Lake Stampede phased out its mountain race in 1954 because the highway got in the way. Sawmills started opening up all over town and in 1956 the schools had to go on double shifts to make room for all the new students. In 1960 they put in dial telephones. The next year they got television, the year after that they got a radio station, and in 1964 the village officially became a town. By 1966, even parts of the Chilcotin country had electricity. Williams Lake got its first mall in 1971, and by that time the stockyards weren't fuelling the economy any more, the lumber mills were. Pretty soon there was no place to pitch a tent down at the rodeo grounds during stampede time, because the lumber yards had taken up all the room.

But life in the Chilcotin country generally went on in the old way. The

Nemiah Valley

Nemiah Valley

Nemiah Valley, looking
north at Mt. Nemiah

Chilko Lake

white people who settled in the country were inclined to look on outsiders with a kind of friendly suspicion, and the Chilcotin Indians had never been much interested in what was happening in the outside world anyway.

In years long past, the Chilcotins tended to live in far-flung bands of extended families that roamed in nomadic cycles deep within their traditional territories, about 25,000 square miles of remote mountain and forest country. It was a way of life that lent itself well to bush ranching, and cattle found an easy place in the old lifestyle, which even now prevails among the Xeni gwet'in more than any other Chilcotin community. Horses also found a cherished place in the Chilcotins' affections, and they remain there to this day. When Simon Fraser came down the river that now bears his name back in the summer of 1808, he found that the Chilcotins were already horsemen (mounted Chilcotins were apparently visiting some Carrier people Fraser encountered at the time).

But the occasional visit and some regular trading was about all the Chilcotins were interested in. For the most part the Chilcotins' diplomatic relations with their neighbours were fleeting, and ranged from cordial to hostile. They were bordered on the north and east by Carrier and Shuswap people, on the south by the Lillooets and on the southwest by the Homathkos. Their nearest western neighbours were the Kwagewlths of the coast, but the high wall of the Coast Range meant they didn't see much if anything of them. On the northwest, they had friends among the Nuxalk, a coastal people from down in the Bella Coola Valley. Apart from that, they kept mostly to themselves and liked it that way, much to the chagrin of the missionaries.

While many of their neighbours embraced Christianity, most Chilcotins simply stuck around during visits from priests long enough to adopt some devotional aspects of Catholicism. Then they'd say so long to Father Morice or Father McGuckin or Father Nobili or whoever happened to be attempting baptisms, mount up, and head back out into the hills again with rosaries in their saddlebags. Catholic traditions are still used occasionally for their healthy, social purposes. Priests are respected, so long as they can be counted on to assist in certain rituals (such as funerals), and icons from the Catholic faith appear in many, if not most, Chilcotin homes. Angels occur in Chilcotin cosmology now and then, and so does the devil, except in Chilcotin folklore

THE BIG CROSS

As told by Eileen William

She was saying that the big crosses were originally put in by the Lord himself and his apostles. She was saying one time long ago when the cross fell down in Bull Canyon, old-timers heard this cross cry out.

She was saying the grandma Annie William told her that these crosses were to be picked back up every time it fell down. They were to get together and pray all day and then put up.

That way the people would have a good life with lots of food and good weather. It would snow starting November and stay until end of March, then it would melt. In springtime it would rain, then summer it would be sunny and rain to keep the grass green, the fall time it would get windy and blow all the leaves away. And people would be more honest. And if they don't put the cross back up the food would be harder to get, the weather would be funny like now at times. It would snow in the middle of summer, rain in winter and get colder at times during spring and it's always windy year round.

She was also saying this person who was putting up the cross, a branch would fall on his back, then it would burn. His helpers would shut it off. And she was saying that they travelled on foot putting up these big crosses along the river towards Chilko River.

Lejab (as Lucifer is known) usually turns up as a white man in a suit. It was only in later years that the Catholic Church's gruesome excesses against Chilcotin people were made public, particularly in cases of physical and sexual abuse that occurred at Saint Joseph's Mission in Williams Lake, where many Chilcotins were interned for schooling.

While the Church had a hard go of it winning converts west of Riske Creek, the Chilcotins' determined independence made things just as difficult for the Hudson's Bay Company, whose traders lamented the Indians' "evil disposition" towards them. Anthropologists have used the word "isolationist" to describe them, and it probably isn't far off the mark. Chilcotins enjoy their own company.

Their language is in arguably better shape than any of the thirty-odd Aboriginal languages in British Columbia. It is a gentle language, but one that requires a gymnastic tongue, and it falls within the Athapascan language family, putting it close to some languages to the north of the Chilcotin but almost as close to the Navajo and Apache of the American southwest. Chilcotin culture, even though it took the same kind of beating that most Indian cultures suffered after British Columbia joined Canada in 1871, took its own course in its own distinct way, with the aid of cattle and horses. By the 1970s the people were undeniably poor, but whatever their pre-contact numbers there were more than 2,000 of them out there still. Most of them can be found without too much difficulty if you're coming from the direction of Williams Lake, on the reserves at Toosey, Anaham, Stoney, Redstone, and Nemiah. That's not counting the old families out in the meadows or the families that settled in up at Alexandria, where the old Hudson's Bay fort was.

So life, such as it was, went on without much interruption from the burgeoning forest industry until around 1980, when the green pine forests began to turn red. Every year, more and more groves of red trees were turning up everywhere.

The old Indians said it was all right, it happened every once in a while. It was just that parts of the forests were dying to make way for new trees and in a matter of time there would be a bad winter and come springtime everything would be back to normal. The trees turned red because of an epidemic of mountain pine beetles, members of a large North American bark beetle family. The beetles lay their eggs in galleries that girdle pine trees, usually trees older than 150 years. The eggs hatch and the larvae eat the tree's phloem layer. Fungus spreads throughout the sapwood. The tree turns red, becomes dry as kindling and eventually goes up in flames. A pine cone usually needs a heat of about 45 degrees celsius to melt the resin that binds its scales together, so after the trees burn the cones pop and start to sprout. The new trees fend off the occupation of the forests by invading tree species, so in its own small way the mountain pine beetle can be credited with the development and maintenance of the Chilcotin's pine forests.

All this made a certain sense to Chilcotin Indians and the white Chilcotin homesteaders that had become their neighbours since about the turn of the century. But the forest companies in Williams Lake saw it as a chance to make their big move on the Chilcotin country, and the provincial government backed the companies all the way.

By 1985, the provincial forest ministry decided to increase the allowable annual cut in the Williams Lake timber supply area from 2.5 million cubic meters a year to 4 million cubic meters year, to "harvest every merchantable stick of wood" wherever a pine beetle could be found. That meant allowing the haul of spruce and fir as well, even though spruce and fir are not susceptible to the pine beetle. Adding in another million cubic meters of wood every year the companies were taking out of privately held lands, the 5 million cubic meters added up to an annual convoy of logging trucks almost 2,000 miles in length, bumper to bumper. Under the guise of beetle-killed pine salvage, the mills in Williams Lake ran round-the-clock shifts, and the government's plan was to keep hammering away at it for five years and keep at it after that unless a 1990 review suggested they should ease up a bit.

When 1988 came around, the beetles died off in a cold winter, just like the old Indians said they would. But the next year, the government decided not only to keep up the accelerated harvest, but to keep up the pace for at least seven years instead of five, and the planned 1990 review was scrapped. Lignum, West Fraser, Jacobsen Brothers, Weldwood and Fletcher Challenge — the big Williams Lake sawmills — were all taking in a total of about 25,000 fully loaded logging trucks a year. But with new technology, they were laying off their workers, not taking new ones on. While the mills' timber consumption soared between 1980 and 1990, the dues-paying woodworkers' union membership shrank from 1,700 to 1,300. Anaham band chief Bernard Elkins watched as a steady convoy of logging trucks roared out the Chilcotin Highway past his reserve, where only three of the band's 650 members had forest industry jobs.

Nobody in the Chilcotin could figure out how to stop it. But it's not that they didn't try.

In 1985, they tried something they'd never really done before, and they actually pulled it off. Guide-outfitters, ranchers, homesteaders, dude ranch operators and trappers, white and Chilcotin, cowboy and Indian, started talking to each other about the country they shared. They set up something called the Chilcotin Survival Coalition and lobbied, prepared reports, conducted surveys, hired consultants, held meetings and circulated petitions all behind the idea that if the logging companies wanted to be part of the Chilcotin they should damn well try to get along with everybody else. The government wasn't listening.

The tribal councils and the Indian bands got together and rallied their white neighbours behind holistic forest licence proposals and community resource boards and integrated management schemes. They even shook up the opposition New Democratic Party in Williams Lake and got a rancher and small logger by the name of Dave Zirnhelt put forward as a candidate in a provincial byelection. He won the election, which was a first for the New Democrats in the Cariboo-Chilcotin, and still the government wasn't listening. The Indians set up roadblocks and organized demonstrations. There was someone up in the Ulkatcho country who was leaving handfuls of tire-popping nails all over the logging roads, but apart from that everything they did was by the book, and by conventional standards they did everything right. But nothing changed. In 1991, the New Democrats swept the old Social Credit regime out of office, and Chilcotin people are still waiting to see whether anything's going to change.

Henry Solomon threw the backwash from his coffee cup into the campfire and shook his head. Tony shook his head. Kelly shook his head and said

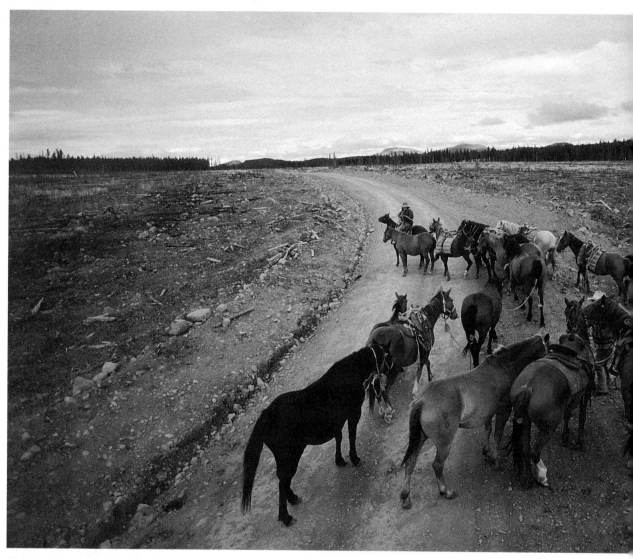

Each year the convoy of
trucks hauling logs out of
the Chilcotin grows, leaving
behind more and more
clearcuts like this one

maybe the Nemiah band's trapping rights case would be the thing to turn it around. Maybe the Nemiah Declaration would do the trick. Some of the clearcuts he'd seen on the way into town left nothing standing at all and in some places it had got so that nothing seemed to be growing anywhere.

"They don't even leave trees for seed," he said.

Henry nodded his head in agreement. He stood up and stretched and said maybe he should go and give Mabel a hand. He walked down towards the beach, stopped, turned and walked back with a grin on his face.

"Already gone," he said. By the time Henry sat back down, Mabel was already rowing the old oar-fitted canoe across the foreshore with her net on her lap.

"You got to move pretty fast to keep up with her, Henry," Tony said.

"Yep," he agreed. "Well, I guess she pretty well knows how to run the ship by herself, I guess."

We heard the lowing of a cow from the swampy meadow behind the trees, across the road from the lakeshore. Kelly looked at Tony, Tony looked at Kelly, and they both laughed.

"Well," Kelly said, "she's in there behind the bog and I guess we're not going to catch her sitting around here."

The two Ahmullicanside cowboys said their goodbyes, mounted up and headed out into the meadows to look for their heifer. Insko and Lhin dozed off again underneath the wagon. Henry walked his horses to the lake's edge to water them before the sun fell below the mountains, and before long Mabel, after setting her net from an overhang further along the beach, pulled the oars slowly back along the shoreline.

The next night, a stout sabay from Mabel's net hung in the alcove of the little one-room cabin where the Solomons passed their days before the long trek to their small herd up the Taseko River.

Henry and Mabel finished their soup and drank some coffee, and we were talking about trees again when Henry mentioned a strange tree that grows at the south end of Chilko Lake. He first saw it about twenty years ago when he was passing through that part of the country. The tree has red bark. It's

Gillnet fishing gear

like a fir tree, only its limbs are high from the ground. There aren't many things that come as a mystery to Henry Solomon, but that tree was one. Another mystery was an animal that used to roam these hills in the old days, like a wolf, but more like a cougar, with a lion's mane.

Mabel turned in to sleep, and Henry and I sat talking in the light of the propane lamp. There were some pots and pans on the old woodstove, some dishes on a makeshift bench and Henry's .22 in its scabbard on the wall, but apart from that most of the Solomons' gear was still in the wagon outside. Not much use in getting too settled since the plan was to hitch up the horses and head out the next day.

Henry was sitting in his jeans and an old checked shirt and talking about his grandmother, Galeen, which is what the Chilcotins make of the name Catherine. She had lived to well over 100 years in age, and I remembered the winter before over at Lhizbay, when Henry first told me about her.

If the death of Samandlin marks the end of the events that came to be known as the Chilcotin War, or at least some crucial juncture in it, then the story of Galeen at Puntzi Lake, or Benziny, as the Chilcotins know the main camp on the lakeshore there, is the beginning.

"Right where they call them lhizqwen, them dugout places. The midugh call them gigilly holes," Henry said. "Gigilly hole" is the way Henry pronounces the term keequeely hole — the remnant pit of semi-subterranean winter houses used by many interior peoples. "That time, everybody die off."

That time, everybody die off. And a strange animal comes out of the woods to feast on those that had died from a disease that the sweathouse could not cleanse away.

No one is sure how many Indians died from the smallpox, or when smallpox drew its first blood on Canada's Pacific coast, but the 1860s epidemic was almost certainly brought by an infected miner who arrived in Victoria from San Francisco, bound for the Cariboo goldfields. When the plague had run its course, whole villages had been decimated all along the coast and well into the interior. Some estimates put the dead at fully half the Indian population west of the Rockies.

The disease found its way quickly into the heart of the Chilcotin country, and the Oblate chronicler Adrian Gabriel Morice reckoned that about two thirds of the Chilcotin people died in its path. A month after the initial outbreak swept through the Indian camps around Victoria, a party of 40 men in the expedition of Francis Poole was making its way from Bella Coola to Alexandria when some of the men fell sick. The people of Anahim Lake took care of them, and within weeks the village was empty but for its rotting corpses. A journalist travelling through the country that summer found 30 abandoned dwellings, many with the dead still inside, and nearby he encountered a survivor who damned the whites who had brought such sickness upon the country. In 1863 Angus McLeod, a trader from the Bella Coola Valley, rekindled the disease. Out of malicious neglect, genocidal intent or simple stupidity, he sold surviving Chilcotins some blankets he had taken from Indian corpses in the bush. The disease again spread throughout the Chilcotin country.

It appears to have been the renewed plague from McLeod's blankets that killed the people at Puntzi, where Galeen was living with her family.

"These white people, they bring blankets, from people who die of small-pox," Henry said. "Then he wrap them up and he sell them to these Indians, then the Indian, he didn't know, he just sleep on it, them blankets. Pretty soon he got them sickness, and pretty soon the whole camp got it. So pretty soon my grandmother and his sister, they're the only one that survive.

"She stayed with them dead bodies one week. She remember real good, and she tell me stories. Emeelee, I guess she's older than my grandmother."

Galeen, from Catherine, and her sister Emeelee, from Emily. Galeen was about seven years old at the time of the smallpox, and her sister Emeelee was a year or two older.

And then the strange animal appears.

"It was just like a lion," Henry said. "Like a lion. Like that. You know, he's got long hair, here," he said, pointing to the back of his neck. "Around the back of his neck.

"They figure he's a wolf, like a nun," pronounced 'noon,' the Chilcotin for wolf. "But my grandmother, she say it's like a nun, because he got long hair here," Henry said, again pointing to the back of his neck.

"He dug out everybody. She say they were all over on the ice. Their bones, everything. He dug them out of the gigilly holes and pulled them over on the ice."

Great horned owl

Timber wolf (nun,
in Chilcotin)

Nobody knew what kind of sickness it was, Henry said. All they knew was that it came from white men, and nothing stopped it. Their spirit power couldn't stop it. The sick would crawl into their sweathouses and come out and bathe in cold water, trying to rid themselves of it, but it was no use.

"It was just like somebody shoot him," he said. "Long time ago, them old-timer Indian he believe that you get sick, you stay in the sweathouse, and he make a mistake when he think he can get rid of the smallpox that way. He just got killed, like flies."

Somehow, the two sisters survived, and they were rescued by someone from a camp at the other end of the lake who had come to visit with Galeen's people.

Galeen raised Henry after Henry's own mother, Mariah, fell ill from tuberculosis, another introduced killer of Indians. Galeen put Henry in the old-fashioned baby baskets the Chilcotin women used to make, and fed him from a milk cow. Henry's father was Timothy, who died one winter during the measles epidemic that swept through Indian communities with a vengeance equalled only by the smallpox.

In the time of his father's death, Henry was living down near Toosey. What he remembers is that every night there came news of four or five more deaths. It was like that here at Xeni Lake, too, on that hill over there, Henry said. The hill above the overhang where Mabel set her net the night before.

"The old-timer people used to live there," he said. "They all die there."

All Henry knew about them was that they used to have horse races on the ice and bet cattle on their races. In the wintertime, the women went fishing for kokanee in horse-drawn sleds.

"Yedanx deni," Henry called them. "Old-timer people."

Henry was still puzzled about the animal that dragged the bones of the dead out over the ice. He said he remembered Raymond Alphonse over at Anaham saying the old people used to tell him the same stories, and it puzzled him, too.

"Do you think a lion would survive a wintertime like that?" Henry asked.

I said mountain lions did, but Henry said no, it wasn't a mountain lion.

"No. Not like that," he said.

"That's what they tell me, that there used to be some kind of lion in the country a long time ago, when the smallpox killed everybody at Benziny."

THE BIG FLU
As told by Eugene William

Eugene said Eagle Lake Henry told him about the big flu that wiped out half of the Chilcotin people in Nemiah and Eagle Lake.

This was in 1918, when Eagle Lake Henry went to hunt over towards Anahim Lake, to get ready for winter. This was in the fall time.

Eagle Lake Henry and his wife were heading back from hunting and stopped to stay a night over Tatla Lake. He talked to a guy staying over Tatla Lake and he told Eagle Lake Henry about the bad sickness going around Eagle Lake. This guy's name was Bob Graham. Bob told Eagle Lake Henry that rum is the best medicine for this sickness. Eugene was saying that rum them days were stronger than the ones nowadays. He said Bob told Eagle Lake Henry the rum was 35 per cent overproof.

Bob told Eagle Lake Henry to drink the rum every once in a while, and he also gave him Lysol. He told Eagle Lake Henry to get a rag and soak it with Lysol and then hang it in your house. So Eagle Lake Henry headed home to Eagle Lake. When he got there he seen all the camps were on high grounds and everyone moved out of their houses. So he went up to the camps to see if his parents were up there, but found out they died from the sickness, so Eagle Lake Henry and his wife went back down to his house near the lake, and he and his wife started to clean out their house. When they cleaned it out they got some rags and soaked it with Lysol and hung them on the walls of the house. Then Eagle Lake Henry and his wife went over to his brother, and found his brother in the house lying on his bed. He was dying, so Eagle Lake Henry bathed him with hot water and poured rum in the tub. Eugene says Eagle Lake Henry's brother got better.

Then Eagle Lake Henry found Nezulhtsin in his underground house. He was very sick from the bad disease that already killed some Chilcotin people. Nezulhtsin was one of the older people. This underground house is built different from a gigilly hole. It has a roof with dirt on top of it, and has a hole where smoke can get through. But it's underground like a gigilly hole, but this one has fire going in it.

Anyway, Eagle Lake Henry got Nezulhtsin to get in a tub of hot water and poured some Lysol in there. Eugene was saying that Nezulhtsin was saying he could see this disease crawling up the steam, and he was starting to feel better already.

Eugene said that in the summer of 1918, John (Eugene didn't know his full name) told the people he wanted to get some lumber from town, Williams Lake, because he wanted a Christmas dance that year, and they couldn't dance on the ground. Back them days there were log houses but there were no floor, just dirt. Eugene said John went to town. Shortly after he left, this disease came from Stone, Eugene was saying. A Chilcotin guy from Nemiah named Tsicone and another person went to Stone and came back with the disease. Eugene told me these two guys were told not to go to Stone because there was a dangerous flu going around there but they still went. So this disease got to Nemiah and wiped out half of the Chilcotins. So this guy Tsicone who came back with the flu felt bad when he found out all his people were dying off from the sickness. He used the lumber John brought from town which was supposed to be for the dance hall until this sickness came around.

Eugene was saying the other Chilcotins didn't help because they were either sick from the disease or to make Tsicone suffer for it. He couldn't see very good. Eugene was saying Tsicone must have been very tough to do all this by himself. But later on the people helped him bury the rest.

After this disease finally quit, Eugene said his father Sammy William's older brother, named Amed, went to Tsuniah where Sammy was staying and told him all about the disease that hit Nemiah. Sammy said he couldn't believe what happened. Surprised, I guess. Because Sammy said he dreamt about this disease. He was dreaming that some soldiers came over to Nemiah and shot this disease with all kinds of colours going through the sky in his dream. That's why Sammy William decided to stay at Tsuniah a little longer.

Eugene was saying that Andy George told him he was 15 years old when the disease hit Nemiah. Eugene was saying the people from there even tried to get a strong medicine man to sing with their sick people from this bad disease but it didn't help any. The medicine man's power was a sunlight shining, which is very strong. Eugene was saying how this medicine man could grab a sunlight shining through a window and hang from it. The medicine man was from Stone and his name was Abiyan.

Eugene said this disease came from the Chilcotin War.

Xeni Lake

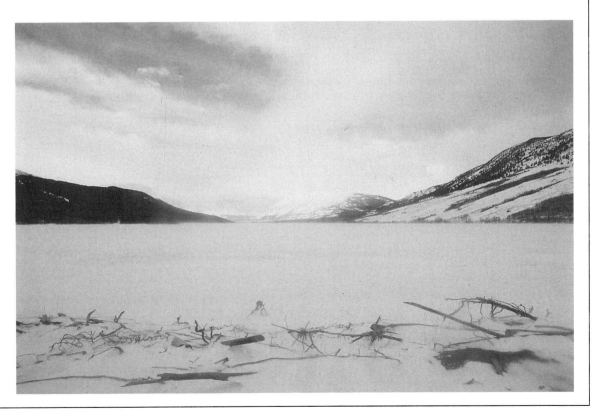

There was another strange animal from the days of the old-timer people, Henry said.

"Something like a big bird," he said, "but it make lots of noise when it's coming. Some kind of yapping, you know. And it had big wings on him. It was a real big bird. Real strong too, I guess. Maybe the devil or something."

That would be the nentŝelghaʔetŝish. It appears to have confined itself to the coast and to the narrow inlets that cut into the mountains of the Xeni gwet'in country from the saltwater. It was known to the Chilcotins who travelled from time to time down the Homathko River to fish, and further downriver to Bute Inlet to trade. Sometimes, a Chilcotin party might winter down on the coast and come back in the springtime, when the snow in the high passes could still be traversed by snowshoe.

"He do trapping, and wintertime down Bute Inlet them bear go all winter. That river there [the Homathko], he used to sell them beaver and the bear hide, that time he sell them down there, to some white people I guess. Long time ago. Mabel's dad used to sell them down there."

The bird gets its name from its reputed habit of sneaking up behind unsuspecting travellers and tearing through their buttocks to get at their entrails. I suggested to Henry that I wouldn't want to meet one of those things.

"No. Me too," he said.

Henry said he knew the coast people were afraid of the nentŝelghaʔetŝish, and the idea was, if you could hear it coming, you hurry to a tree and stand with your back to it so the bird couldn't attack.

Henry said he couldn't imagine what kind of an animal it was.

"Could you think of what that's like, Terry? Do you know what the hell it is?"

The only thing that came to mind was a supernatural creature the people on the coast were long familiar with, represented in dances by huge cedar masks depicting a long-beaked bird. It caught the imagination of people throughout the coast, whatever it was.

"I guess them guys, they know. They should know," Henry said. "Those guys who lived around the coast. How about Vancouver Island, them Indians? Did they ever hear of a big bird like that?"

So far as I could recall, Vancouver Island people were aware of it, too.

The coast was where it was seen, Henry remembered. Down the Homathko Canyon, and down into Bute Inlet.

"That's where you see him, long time ago," he said.

In Chilcotin stories, the Homathko Canyon was often a source of dread. It was from the darkness of the Homathko Canyon that a party of warriors from the coast emerged in the days of the old-timer people. It was summertime. The Xeni gwet'in were in the nearby mountains digging wild potatoes.

"Must have been sometime in July, like," Henry said. "They'd be down by Potato Mountain. Chunaẑch'ez. Potato Mountain."

The women were up in the alpine digging the root that was a staple in the Xeni gwet'in diet and the men were off hunting, probably for black bear. The Bute Inlet Indians crept up the mountainside and slaughtered all but two of the women, who were taken as captives. But there was a young boy who witnessed the slaughter, and he hurried away to tell what had happened.

By the time the boy met up with the hunters, the attackers were well on their way back to their home territory, so the deyen, as the shaman is known in Chilcotin, began to sing.

"He started to sing, you know," Henry said. "And then pretty soon he get a bird sitting right on his hand. A kingfisher, so he just blow on it, and the bird, he started making noise, and the bird just took off down to catch the people before he get to the coast down there.

"There's a big rock wall along the edge, along the side of that river. One way out, and one way in."

The Bute Inlet war party saw the kingfisher, but didn't think anything of it.

Back in the mountains, the deyen told the kingfisher to make the attackers fall asleep. While they slept, the Chilcotin hunters caught up to them and traversed the alpine above the canyon, just below the timberline. The Bute Inlet party was trapped inside the canyon and the Chilcotins surprised them in their sleep, freeing the two women and killing all but two of the Bute Inlet party. The pair of survivors made it back to the village that later became known as Church House, but the deyen was not through with them. One survivor told his story, and after he was finished, blood gushed from his mouth and he died. The same kind of death took the second survivor.

It was also out of the Homathko Canyon, the year after the wolf with a lion's

mane dragged the corpses out onto the ice at Benziny, that Waddington's road crew emerged. It was 1864.

Until 1864, white adventurers, prospectors and exploring expeditions were tolerated by the Chilcotins. Poole's party had been assisted by the Chilcotins he met along the way, and in the early days of Waddington's grand scheme of a better route to the gold mines of the Cariboo district, some Chilcotins wintered down on the coast as labourers, guides and packers.

But by the summer of 1864, everything had changed. The Chilcotins were acutely aware of the military use of magic, as the singing deyen had used his hummingbird power, and the smallpox in the whites' arsenal was a form of magic that none of the old medicines could prevail against. These people were already streaming in their hundreds through the Shuswap country to the east, and while in the past they had remained beyond the Chilcotins' frontiers, now they were coming in from the southwest out of the Homathko Canyon, and from the northwest from the Bella Coola Valley.

It was from the Bella Coola Valley that Angus McLeod had come with his smallpox blankets. And it was from the Bella Coola Valley that a group of speculators was already laying the groundwork for another road project through the Chilcotin country to the goldfields. That road proposal was known in the colonial capitals of Victoria and New Westminster as the Bentinck Arm route, and its financiers were racing against Waddington and his roadbuilders down at Bute Inlet.

Down in Waddington's work camps in the spring of 1864, half-starved Chilcotins with smallpox scars on their faces had begun to show up looking for hunting muskets and food in return for their labour. The artist Frederick Whymper noted that some of the Chilcotins were living on scraps thrown from the white workers' camp tables, and road foreman William Brewster was known to throw the scraps into the fire rather than feed hungry Chilcotins. Chartres Brew, British Columbia's chief police inspector, noted that Brewster "gave them nothing to eat" even though "it was known that the Indians were little removed from a state of starvation." Brew said the Chilcotins were reduced to begging, and their young women prostituted themselves for food. As soon as a Chilcotin earned enough by packing for a musket and some blankets, he would leave the canyon and its camps.

With dozens of hungry smallpox survivors lurking in the bush, some flour was stolen from a storehouse. One of the roadbuilders, almost certainly Brewster, wrote down the names of a group of Chilcotins and told them he would bring smallpox back into the country to punish them for what they had done.

More than 100 miles away, at Puntzi Lake, another man — one of two partners in a packing venture with a Waddington contract — had somehow, singlehandedly, driven off Galeen's rescuers and built a rough cabin at a site which would have made a perfect waystation on the route from Bute Inlet to Alexandria. His name was William Manning. Judge Matthew Begbie later pointed out in a letter to colonial governor Frederick Seymour that a white man in the Chilcotin country had threatened to return the smallpox to the Indians. Manning was the only white settler in the Chilcotin country at the time.

It is at this point in the story that a Chilcotin with the name Lhasas?in, which means 'we don't know who it is,' appears. The missionary Lundin Brown says Lhasas?in was "looked upon as their chief" by all the Chilcotins and was so fearsome that children would run in fear at the sight of him. Judge Begbie described Lhasas?in as "the finest savage I have met with yet, I think." Not much more is known about him, but he had arrived in the Homathko country with a small band of men, some women and children. There were perhaps twelve men in Lhasas?in's company, judging by the various court depositions and investigation reports that followed, including Lhasas?in's own account. Among them were Lhasas?in's son, Piell, a friend, Cheddeki, Chessus, Cusshen, Chrayanuru, and Llowa. But it was without doubt Lhasas?in who was in control of the events which were to follow, and as he said before his death on the gallows, he had come down the Homathko to make war.

The first to die was a ferryman, Tim Smith, who was assigned to guard the cable crossing, about 30 miles from saltwater. On April 29, 1864, he was shot from a distance, and the stores he guarded — hundreds of pounds of supplies, including food, two kegs of gunpowder and thirty pounds of musket balls — were looted. The scow ferry was destroyed, cutting off a group of workers and an advance party further up the Homathko.

The next morning, at dawn, Lhasas?in and his men descended on the work camp. Within minutes, Charles Butler, John Newman, James Oppenshaw, Alexander Millan, George Smith, John Hoffman, Robert Pollock, Joseph

Fielding and James Campbell were dead. The nine workmen were shot, hacked to pieces and clubbed to death. Three men escaped: Philip Buckley, Edward Mosley and Peter Petersen.

Within hours, Lhasas?in and the others walked into the camp of Brewster's advance party about two miles further upriver. A Homathko Indian who was working for Brewster was alone in the camp. The others were on ahead.

Within minutes, four more men were dead. They were Baptiste Demerest, John Clark, Jim Gaudet and finally Brewster, the man who threatened to bring the smallpox back into the country after he discovered some flour missing. Brewster was found with a musket ball in his chest and his head smashed open. Some reports had him castrated, with his heart cut out. The Homathko boy was allowed to run away.

A few days later, Lhasas?in's party had reached the camp of Chief Anaham, whose village on the shores of Anahim Lake had been turned into a ghost town two years earlier during the first wave of the smallpox. Shortly after Lhasas?in's arrival, a member of Chief Anaham's band named Tahpitt, armed with a musket and a hatchet, walked across the meadows near Puntzi Lake towards William Manning's cabin. Manning had been warned by his Chilcotin wife that there was going to be trouble, but the local Indians had worked for him, helped him clear his fields, and he wasn't all that concerned. Tahpitt found him in a meadow, aimed his musket and fired a ball that shot clear through Manning and brought him to the ground. Tahpitt then took the hatchet to Manning's face. A group of men and women who had followed behind Tahpitt plundered Manning's cabin, smashed his meagre equipment and dumped his body in a nearby creek.

By May 17, Manning's partner, Alexander McDonald, was already making his way into the Chilcotin country from Bella Coola at the head of a pack train consisting of 42 pack animals carrying goods worth more than $4,000. With him were eight white men and a Chilcotin guide named Tom. Among the white men was a packer named Peter McDougall, who was bringing along his Chilcotin wife, Klymtedza, for the trip to Alexandria. As for McDonald, he intended to meet up with Manning at Puntzi Lake to begin work on Waddington's road from there, blazing it back southwest towards the Homathko Canyon.

By the time McDonald's pack train had reached the summit of a place called the Great Slide and was making its first few miles into Chilcotin country, it was becoming clear that something was wrong. McDougall's wife, Klymtedza, said their lives were in danger because of plans she had heard about for a general uprising against the whites. By the time the pack train reached Anahim Lake, Lhasasʔin had already been there, recruiting warriors and laying plans to ambush McDonald somewhere between Nimpo Lake and Puntzi Lake.

A few miles past Anahim Lake, McDonald's party called it quits. They constructed a rude earthworks fort on a knoll that commanded a view of the surrounding meadows. Their guide, Tom, was sent out to look for two missing pack horses. When he didn't return, McDonald decided to turn back.

At this point, the pack train consisted of 40 horses, eight white men and an Indian woman. After the party had covered a mere five miles of the trail back to Bella Coola, it was attacked from both sides. The horses panicked, the white men bolted in every direction, and Peter McDougall was the first to get hit.

The dead were McDougall, Klymtedza, Clifford Higgins, and McDonald, who fired a fatal shot at the warrior Chacatinea before his own death. The five surviving whites, bleeding and battered, made their way the remaining 100 miles back to Bella Coola on foot.

Apart from some injuries sustained during skirmishing with the 50-man expeditionary force led by William Cox, there was no blood shed in direct engagements until the killing of Samandlin several weeks later. But Chacatinea's death had its own consequences, resulting in the murder-suicide of two of his brothers, identified as Niko and Chinanihim.

Henry Solomon tells the story this way. There was a man who didn't want to make war anymore, and his brother killed him because of it. The murderer, so full of remorse, had his friends build a great bonfire for him, and he threw himself into the flames.

"Yep," Henry said. "Used to be like that."

In Chilcotin, war is deni ts'ulhdilh.

To get ready for deni ts'ulhdilh, you build a big campfire, dance around it, and sing.

Benny Lulua
playing lahal

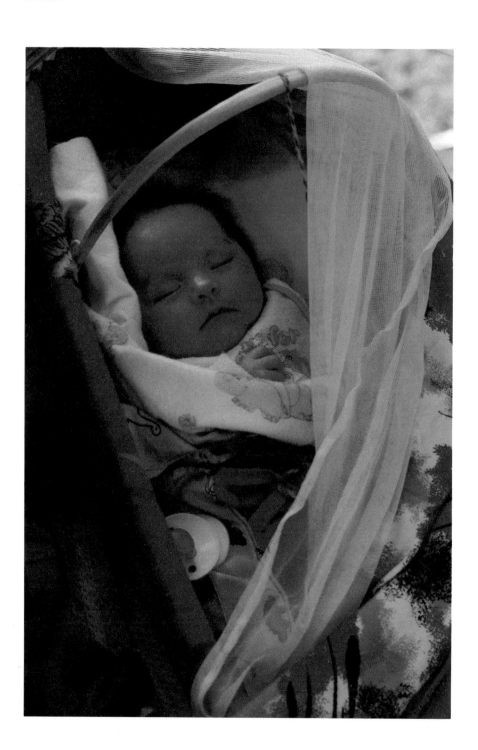

Nicole Setah

Annie Setah, haying

Emily Ekks

Juliana Setah at fish camp

"They maybe get some of them wild spuds and something like that," Henry said. "Kind of a party, like.

"Some paint up themselves, maybe put some kind of like a groundhog hide on his head. Some of them put feathers on his head. On top of his head. I guess he gotta wear some kind of old-timer clothes, then he dance like that. So he dance like that, before he go to war."

In the days before smallpox and muskets, war was not carried out on a grand scale. It was undertaken by small groups of men.

"They use them spear and that bow and arrow, stuff like that," Henry said. "They used to war with them rock, with a sinew on it. That one, they knock you on the head. They just kill you like that."

Or with kingfisher medicine, as the deyen had used in the war with the Bute Inlet people, or with the hummingbird. The ts'utanchuny.

One of the old-timer people, a witch doctor, was headed down to Gwetsilh, the place known as Siwash Bridge down in Bull Canyon, Henry explained. Someone kidnapped his wife during the salmon run, and the witch doctor caught sight of him on the other side of the river. The witchdoctor dreamed about the ts'utanchuny, the hummingbird, and started to sing.

"Pretty soon you see this hummingbird sitting on his hand, and he just blew on it, and it flew right through that fella, on the back, and he just dropped right there, dead."

The Chilcotins needed powers like that, considering their powerful neighbours. Border fights and retaliatory raids weren't common, but they weren't unheard of, either.

To the south, there were the the Lillooets, known to the Chilcotin as the ?Eŝch'ed. Now and then the Chilcotins would engage ?Eŝch'ed hunting parties during the Chilcotins' journeys to pick saskatoon berries in the mountains above Shalalth. It was just such an encounter that gave Graveyard Valley its name, from the Chilcotin 'deni dildzan.'

On the eastern frontiers there were the Shuswap, the ?Ena. The Farwell Canyon ?Ena were friends to the Chilcotin, but the rest were not. "They start down that way and they sneak up here and try to kill all the Chilcotin," Henry said, "and the Chilcotin, he do the same thing."

BULL CANYON WAR
As told by Danny Sammy

At Bull Canyon there was a war between Chilcotins and Shuswaps. The Chilcotins cornered the Shuswaps at Bull Canyon and killed all of them except their one medicine man. He was very strong. They cornered him on the edge of Bull Canyon cliff. Then this medicine man jumped off the cliff and landed across the river and let out a yell and turned into smoke. I guess that's why they call the tall rocks there a big cigar. Anyway, a Chilcotin medicine man followed him and caught up with the Shuswap medicine man and chased him until he crossed the Fraser River. He never came back across again.

Then there were the Homathko Indians of Bute Inlet, known to the Xeni gwet'in as Qaju, with whom there were rarely if ever good relations.

The ʔEnay of the Bella Coola Valley were long-time friends of the Chilcotin, and they used to invite the Chilcotins down from the mountains into the valley to spend the winters with them for their long winter ceremonials. Henry had never heard of any scraps with ʔEnay.

In the north there were the various Carrier tribes, like the Sut'in and the Nichat'in, and other, more mysterious people who were rumoured to steal children from the more remote camps.

"Long time ago, you know, some tall Indians, they come," Henry said. "Maybe them Cree Indians, you think? Tall people?"

It wasn't clear who they were, but they were known to the Carriers as well.

"They come here and they steal a bunch of young people and they take them back thataway," Henry said, adding that the Chilcotins never got a chance to make war with them, which, by the sound of things, was fortunate for the tall people, whoever they were.

Sometime around the end of the 19th century, the people were growing particularly tired of the constant threat of war. So, the Chilcotins and their neighbours put generations of hostility behind them one summer in a sort of intertribal peace conference. It must have been around the late 1800s, since Charlie Quilt from Stoney was there when he was a little boy, and so was John Baptiste, from Nemiah.

"That old man Sammy and John Baptiste, he told me all that story," Henry said. "That's why I don't forget all that happened down there. Because they tell me all that story."

What happened down there, up in the Snow Mountains, was the Chilcotins and the Shuswaps and the Lillooets took hundreds of years of hostility and gambled it all away in horse races, wrestling matches and lahal.

"Anyway," Henry went on, "they decided, 'no more war.' And at night time, they played lahal. The Shuswap, the Chilcotin, the Lillooets. All night they play that.

"Daytime, they race horses, they do wrestling and everything like that, and foot races. Anybody, you know. Good man, they box. Chilcotin and Shuswap.

That Lillooet Indian, he pick out a good man and try to beat out Shuswap and Chilcotin. See how strong, who's the best man. Wrestling, boxing, foot races."

Apparently it was the Lillooets' idea. There were Lillooets who were familiar with chinook. The Shuswaps were certainly familiar with it, it's about all they ever talked around Fort Kamloops, and in later years the Oblates ran a newspaper out of Shuswap country in the chinook jargon. Some Chilcotins were familiar enough with it to get by, and some of the older people these days still are.

"So some Lillooet people, he invite all the Chilcotin. I guess some way he brought that letter, so he read them, and then them Shuswap . . . he write to these people on Alkali Lake and Dog Creek and them people. We all go together over there with Lillooet Indians. We all go together, like that, so finally he don't want no more war."

It was down in the Snow Mountains, just on the Chilcotin side of a place known as Tŝichaghinlin, on the way down into the Bridge River country where the beartooth root grows on the alpine.

"Old Johnny Quilt wrestled one of those Lillooet Indians," Henry said. "He threw him right up in the air, spin, up on top, put him right down on the ground, put him flat on your back. Then you win.

"We call him Bigad, in Chilcotin. That Johnny Quilt. He win everybody. Those Lillooet Indian, them Shuswap.

"No more war since then," Henry said.

No such peaceable intentions prevailed in the camp of Cox's expeditionary force on August 15, 1864, when Lhasasʔin and his warriors agreed to come in and talk terms with the colonial authorities.

The fighting couldn't go on forever. Lhasasʔin's warriors and their families were constantly on their guard, even after Samandlin was killed. The Chilcotin bands were continually harassed by the demands of the white mercenaries. The warrior families could not attend their fishing sites without fear of attack — they had to take care even with the smoke from their fires. To make matters worse, Cox's 50 men had been joined by another expedition of 40 men, led by Chartres Brew and Governor Seymour himself.

*On the west side
of Chilko Lake*

The warriors made contact with Cox, through a son of Tahpitt, who had killed Manning. They proposed a meeting.

Cox later maintained that he had advised Tahpitt's son that Lhasasʔin's arrival would be regarded as his surrender, but that was clearly not Lhasasʔin's understanding of the meeting's purpose.

From Cox's account, it would appear that Lhasasʔin arrived early in the morning with seven other warriors, unarmed. He presented Cox with a horse, a mule and $20 for Governor Seymour, whom he apparently expected to meet.

The seven rebels with Lhasasʔin were his son Piell, who participated in the attack on the work crew on the Homathko and the pack train near Anahim Lake; Chessus, Tellot and Cheddeki, who were participants in the Homathko raid; Tahpitt, who killed Manning; and Sanstanki and his son Cheloot, whose roles were so unclear that they were released.

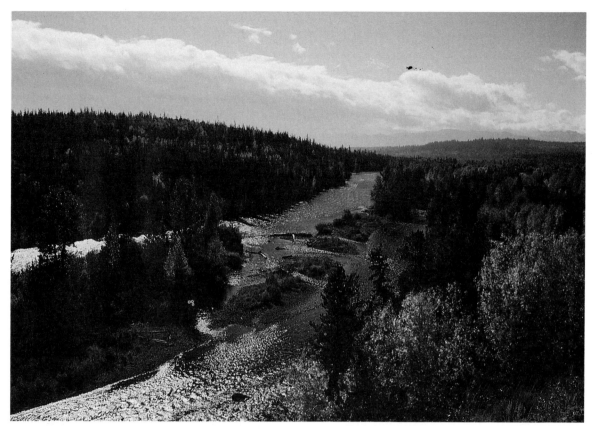

Chilko River

Cox said that Lhasas?in, through an interpreter, told him on the morning of August 15 that there had been 21 rebels all told. Eight were present, three rebels were dead — Chacatinea and the two brothers — and ten others were still in the mountains. He named them as Setah (whose name comes up often and is regarded by many Chilcotins as a key participant in some fashion), Quotanuski, Ahan, Yahooslas, Yeltenly, Hachis, Cusshen, Katelth, Anukatlk (named in some reports as Samandlin's killer) and Lutas.

Before any discussions took place, Lhasas?in and his seven comrades were arrested at gunpoint. The Chilcotins were stunned. Tellot is said to have flown into a rage, and Chief Alexis, who had acted as a sort of an intermediary between Cox and the rebels in arrangements for the meeting, is said to have accused the colonial authorities of being great liars.

Despite the controversy that raged in the colonial press, five of the 21 named rebels — Lhasasʔin, Piell, Tahpitt, Chessus and Tellot — were taken from their cells at Quesnellesmouth on the morning of October 26, 1864, and hanged.

Another rebel remained in custody. Cheddeki was to be tried in New Westminster, where one of the Homathko survivors, Peter Petersen, was said to be capable of identifying him as one of the attackers. But on the way to New Westminster, Cheddeki escaped.

The only further arrests made were those of Ahan and Lutas, who turned themselves in down in Bella Coola the following year. Their hopeless plan was apparently to buy some kind of pardon with the hundreds of dollars' worth of furs they had obtained after a long winter's trapping. But it was Chief Anaham who encouraged them to give up, and he may well have considered it best for the whole community if these two sacrificed themselves. Whatever the case, they were charged with McDougall's murder during the attack on McDonald's pack train. They were brought down to New Westminster and put on trial, and on July 4, 1865, they were sentenced to death. Governor Seymour pardoned Lutas, because "there has been enough life sacrificed already," but Ahan was hanged on July 15.

As for Cheddeki the escaper, Henry recalls a warrior who was captured and later escaped, but that warrior was known as Ŝumayu, or something close to that pronunciation, which adds to the ever-present mystery about who exactly was who in the Chilcotin War, starting with the alleged war leader, Lhasasʔin ('we don't know who it is').

Ŝumayu is said to have walked all the way back into the Nemiah country, and he spent the rest of his days as a trapper in the Snow Mountains. His guardian spirit, or the animal from which he drew his power, was the magpie.

"He got away," Henry said. "That's the fella who came back all the way here. He live way back in there, maybe Yohetta, so people can't find him. Only a few people know where he camp."

By Henry's account, he was pursued for a time as a fugitive, but nobody could catch him.

"That magpie, you know. That's his witch doctor, like. Somebody coming towards him, he knows they're coming. He just goes up a mountain, slides down a bluff. You can't catch him. No way."

When Ŝumayu, or Cheddeki, grew old, he came back down from the

SETAH SINGS WITH SAMMY WILLIAM

As told by Danny Sammy

Setah was a very strong medicine man. The beaver was his power and that would be, I would guess, the strongest power, if not one of the strongest. Setah wanted Sammy William, our grandfather (Danny's father) to become a medicine man. Anyway, one time there was a gathering in Redstone with the priest, and Sammy and his family went over there. When they got there he went to join his friends and one of them slapped him on the back and it scared Sammy so much he got very sick. He barely made it home, then somebody, or person, don't know his or her name, must've went and got Setah to sing with Sammy.

So Setah sang with Sammy and told him when he got slapped in the back his power (a red beaver) dove under the water with him. That's why he got so sick. Anyway, Setah brought the beaver back up and took Sammy off. Then Sammy got better. So Sammy told Setah, "Why are you doing this to me?" I guess he meant, why are you trying to make me a medicine man in your power. So I guess Setah didn't give him his power. But Danny figures Sammy still had that red beaver for his power because he was saying he sure worked like one.

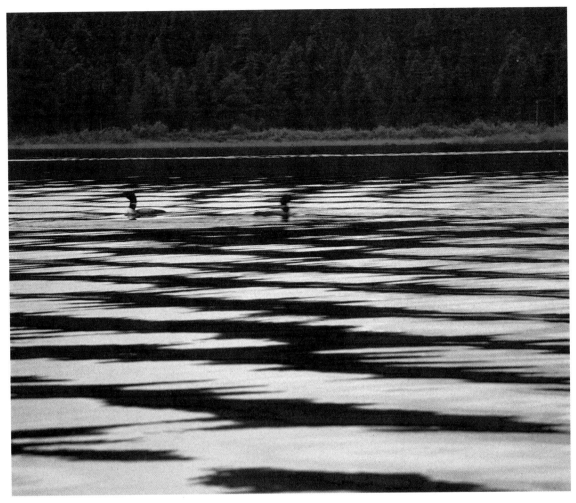

Loons

mountains into the Nemiah Valley and lived down where Marvin Baptiste's house is now, and that's where he's buried.

Then there's Setah, or Sit'ax. He is always referred to as a powerful witch doctor, and some stories have him arguing with angels. Others have him trying to rehabilitate Chilcotins who were taking on some Catholic attributes. His power came from the beaver, and Henry said that long before the Chilcotin War, he had been captured as a child by the Homathko people, was raised down at the seacoast, and returned to the Chilcotin country to take up with Lhasas?in only after an old Homathko told him where he was from. He is said to have known stories about the nentŝelgha?etŝisish, the giant bird that Henry reckons might be the devil himself.

"But Sit'ax, he's from Nemiah Valley," said Henry. Setah is still one of the Nemiah's most common names, and probably half the Xeni gwet'in count Sit'ax among their grandfathers, great-uncles or great-grandfathers.

When all is said and done, nineteen white men were killed. A Chilcotin woman, married to a white man, was also killed. Only one Chilcotin warrior died in action. Two died in a related murder-suicide. Six of the 21 Chilcotin warriors Lhasas?in named during his meeting with Cox were hanged.

The Bentinck Arm route foundered with the attack on McDonald's pack train and never got built. After the attack on the Homathko, the Bute Inlet route was abandoned in a hurrah of stock-price chaos and political upheaval, and never got built.

Alfred Waddington died in Ottawa on February 26, 1872. Cause of death: smallpox.

The warriors of 1864 returned to the Xeni gwet'in mountains, raised children and continued in control of their destiny. The Xeni gwet'in remained unconquered.

"Chilcotins, they never got beat," Henry said with a smile. He stood up, laughed, and pushed another piece of split wood into his stove. "Never got beat."

FRANCIE LULUA GETS A FRIDGE

The Thanksgiving Day winds roared across Chilko Lake, bending and twisting the tall pines along the shore. The signs of an early, cold winter were all there. Everyone else was working hard to put in their hay.

William Lulua's got his hay in, but he's the only one. William Setah's still haying, and so is Ronny Solomon, Eugene William and Roger William. Almost all the families, with their small herds of 30 or 40 head at most, have been a little worried about the winter coming in so quick. The squirrels were putting in their conepiles early everywhere, and back in the summer people noticed how the beehives were high above the ground, not like most years when they're in rotting wind-downed trees.

Francie Lulua stood in the corner of her small, one-room cabin, tucked away in a stand of pines and birch on the shores of Chilko Lake. Beside Francie stood a half-sized, propane-fueled fridge, a Frigiking Astral. She opened the fridge door with her left hand and put her right hand inside.

"It's getting cold now," she said, closing the door. She's had a propane tank for nearly two years, but this morning, after she'd been out riding and admiring a rainbow over the lake before the winds came up, the two Scotts from Del's Propane in Williams Lake arrived and installed a second propane lamp and this fridge.

"I didn't ever have a fridge before," she said, staring at the contraption. "This is my first time."

She got along fine without one, she said, but the band office was trying to make life a little better for its members, so propane fridges were starting to show up these days in the tiny houses throughout the Nemiah Valley. Before, 24-year-old Francie and her kid sister Lillian would put perishables in the open space under their sink, where they usually stayed cold enough.

Her cabin boasts two beds, a couch, a woodstove, a hot water tank that runs off the stove, a table and some chairs. She has a cat named Boosie, which is the Chilcotin for cat, and another cat named Weasel. There's Rex the dog that barks a lot and three more dogs that don't bark so much. She and her sister have eight horses, two steers, a heifer and a milk cow between them, and they don't have much use for a vehicle because they get around by saddle horse.

We sat and looked at the fridge and talked.

"I had a fawn one time," Francie said. "Had him in here with me. He'd sleep under the bed, and when I was sleeping he used to come and wake me up. Harry Setah shot his mother by mistake, so I raised him for a while, but he died on me."

Rex runs into the house, barking. She tells him to be quiet, in Chilcotin, and stares out the window.

"This is my favourite spot," she said. "It feels like a real home here, and the bears don't come too close."

Her white dog chases them off, and sometimes comes home with a proud look on his face and clumps of bear fur in his mouth.

She's got everything she needs, she says.

"Cousins come by and visit. It's nice."

She's just finished helping her parents put in their winter hay, and she likes that kind of work. She nets dolly varden and rainbow trout from the lake in the springtime to eat fresh or to smoke, and later in the summer she wind-dries the salmon she catches.

She looked at the fridge some more.

"They were asking us if we were excited," she said, thinking about Scott and Scott from Del's Propane. "I guess we were."

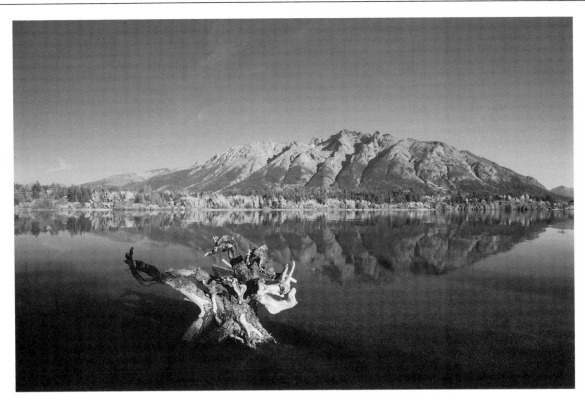

Looking west across

Chilko Lake

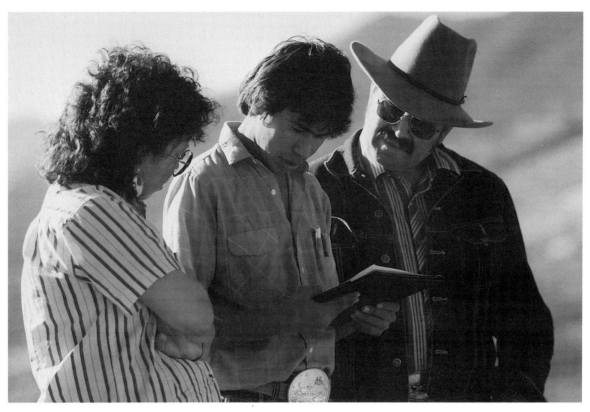

*Annie Williams, Roger
William, and Bennie
William — the last three
Nemiah band chiefs*

CHAPTER 3

BENNY, ANNIE AND ROGER

The Third Field Squadron of the Canadian military engineers finished the first 20 miles of the Stoney-Nemiah road in November, 1966. By the summer of 1967, the engineers had pushed through another 17 miles, and by the end of the summer of 1969, the first vehicles crossed the Davidson Bridge over the Taseko River. The final 22 miles, past Xeni Lake to the shores of Chilko Lake, were completed by July 1973.

After the Chilcotin War, the first chief of the Xeni gwet'in known to the outside world was Chief Nemiah. He was followed by ʔAchig, Seal Canim, Lashaway Lulua, Henry Solomon, Danny William, Marvin Baptiste and Adam William.

The Nemiah Valley Indian band is one of the few remaining Indian bands in B.C. that still conducts its political business "by custom" rather than by Indian Affairs Department rules. The Nemiah people hold elections, generally every two years, but they don't ask civil servants to come all the way out to make fools of themselves counting votes. They just tell Ottawa who the chief is and who the councillors are, and by the mid-1980s the band leadership had fallen to Benny William, Annie Williams and Roger William.

Benny William is a big man. He's 46 now, and he's got a big family. He and his wife Maryanne have four children — Chris, 20, Barbie, 18, Janet, 16, and Linda, 12. Benny was the fourth of Eugene and Mabel William's twelve children, and they grew up five miles down a wagon road from Henry's

Crossing on the Chilko River. There was no bridge at Henry's Crossing then, just a shallow stretch where the horses could be run across.

The way in to the family's meadow was by horse and wagon, or sleigh in the wintertime, and Benny remembers those days as the best of his life. He dreams about those days still, about when the whole family would head out to Potato Mountain to dig wild spuds, and he remembers the deep grass, the wildflowers, and that one evening when he counted 30 deer on the mountainside.

Benny's brothers and sisters were Juliana, Agnes, Catherine, Nelson, Boysie, Evan, Alice, Raphael, Leona, Hank and June. It was full-time work keeping them clothed and fed. When they reached school age, Eugene and Mabel didn't just send the kids off to school — it wasn't that easy back then. Eugene had to build a cabin for his children in Tatlayoko, within walking distance of Tatlayoko's old one-room schoolhouse. It was tough on the family. It was hard for the kids to learn how to speak English. But what was good about it was the kids didn't have to be packed off to the mission school, Saint Joseph's, in Williams Lake. They stayed in Tatlayoko, lived on deer meat and wild potatoes, and cut firewood with a crosscut saw. After Benny finished his schooling at the Roman Catholic school and the college in Prince George, he joined his family down in the Nemiah Valley. After five years as chief, Benny stepped down to make way for Annie Williams, who began her three-year term in 1988.

Annie was a bright girl, the oldest of seven children who lived the old way, back in the Tatlayoko country. Annie Williams packed firewood, scraped hides, cleaned fish, and dried meat. Because she was the oldest her parents, Ubill and Juliana, figured Annie should be something of a role model to the others, and Annie all but raised her brothers and sisters. When they weren't out in the meadows putting in the hay or hunting in the mountains, the family lived in a log house in the Tatlayoko Valley. It was when she was a baby, around Easter time, that Eagle Lake Henry, her grandfather, pointed it out to her parents. She was crawling on the floor.

She would turn out to be something, Eagle Lake Henry had said, and they always remembered what he had to say. She was going to do something important. When she reached school age, Benny took Annie under his arm and off they went to Tatlayoko's one-room schoolhouse. Annie is the first to

KA K'US

As told by Eugene William

Eugene was saying that Ka K'us was his mother Annie Sammy-William's grandfather and Eagle Lake Henry's dad.

Eagle Lake Henry told Eugene about this story. Eugene was saying Eagle Lake Henry said he was a kid when he and Ka K'us went down Chilko River in a cutout canoe. Then they head off down the river and Eagle Lake Henry said they seen a bear on the hillside so they went to shore. Ka K'us got out and shot the bear down, and they went over to check the bear and found out there was another with him. So Ka K'us told Eagle Lake Henry that this bear will come back, so they slept overnight away from the dead bear where they can see it. Sure enough the other bear came back that morning and Ka K'us shot him, Eagle Lake Henry said to him. Ka K'us cut up the bear into pieces and loaded them onto the cutout canoe and headed up the river. Then they shored at Canoe Crossing which is at the end of Chilko Lake. Them days Eugene was saying people loved bear meat (black bear). He said if you don't share the meat among the Chilcotins, the medicine man will get you very sick or even kill you with his powers, because back in them days you were lucky to even see a black bear.

So when Eagle Lake Henry and Ka K'us got the bear meat hung up, Eagle Lake Henry said you see all the Chilcotin Indians coming from the hillside. So Ka K'us cooked, fried and baked all the bear meat for the people. Eugene said the two bears Eagle Lake Henry and Ka K'us killed were eaten up in one day. Eugene said Eagle Lake Henry told him Ka K'us was good at that kind of thing, sharing.

Boysie William, a trapper

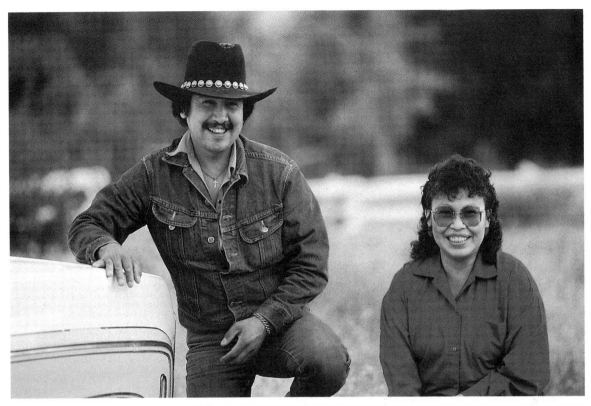

Walter Lulua and
Annie Williams

Roger William

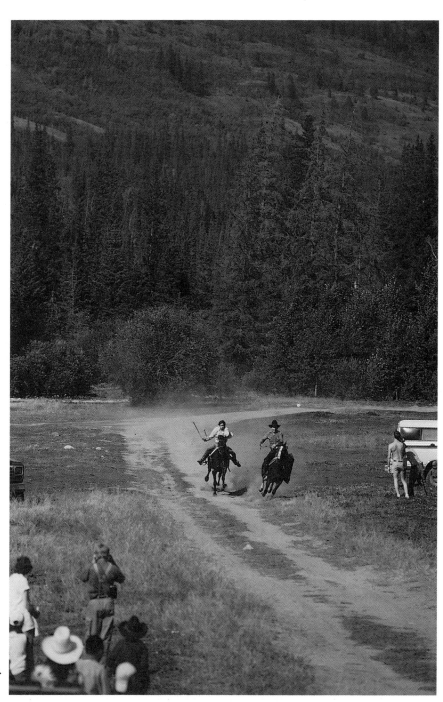

The 1990 mountain race,
which Roger William won.
He is on the left.

admit that it's been rough going. She's the first woman to be chief of the Nemiah band, and she's been a wife and mother at the same time, during one of the most difficult periods in the band's history. So it was almost a relief when her term was up and Roger William took over.

Roger's 27, the youngest of the three. He's a rodeo rider. He's done the Chilcotin Rodeo Association circuit since he was a kid. His strength is bullriding. His lucky rodeo ground is Riske Creek.

Roger was born at Naghataneqed, the grove of birch at the far end of Xeni Lake where Henry sat and told stories by his campfire. When he was a boy, Roger travelled with his family back and forth across the broad valley, moving with the cattle, trapping squirrels for $2 a pelt, gaffing salmon out at Henry's Crossing, and living the old life.

He went to Saint Joseph's for kindergarten and Grade 1, then he was sent to Saint Mary's Mission at Kamloops Mission, then back to the new Nemiah Valley school from Grades 3 to 9, then Columneetza in Williams Lake, and finally to Chilliwack to finish high school. Along the way, Roger says, he's learned a few things, and one of those things is that you don't throw away what you're going to need.

"You cut down all the trees, maybe it won't even come back. The lakes will be drying up, drying off. The runoff will move a lot of land, destroy the soil. The ranchers depend on the land, and if the land won't hold the rain, it'll all dry off. Ranching's been here three generations now. We don't want to lose that, either.

"A lot of our future will be history. We want to preserve the way we live, for our kids. If you don't disturb the nature, you can do it all the time, because the nature knows, and it does what it needs to do."

And for all that had changed in almost 130 years since the Chilcotin War, life in the Nemiah country still goes on in many ways as it always has. The people still hunt, trap, fish and follow their small herds of bush cattle through the heavily forested mountains. But the outside world still poses a threat, and by the mid-1980s, it was clear that something had to be done about it.

In the autumn of 1985, Annie and Walter and the kids packed up and headed to Chilliwack, where Annie had enrolled in the two-year business administration program at Fraser Valley College. It was during a visit home

THE HORSES THAT WENT TO HEAVEN

As told by Danny Sammy

Over at Mountain House, he was saying, Eagle Lake Henry had his horse in his pasture. Eagle Lake Henry must've come back from hunting or fishing or something and noticed his horse wasn't in the pasture. He looked all over but all he seen was tracks in the pasture, not outside the pasture. It was weird, he was saying. He figures the horses must have gone to heaven.

Wild horses in the
Chilcotin bush

Nemiah Valley Rodeo

ʔEniyud (Niut Range)

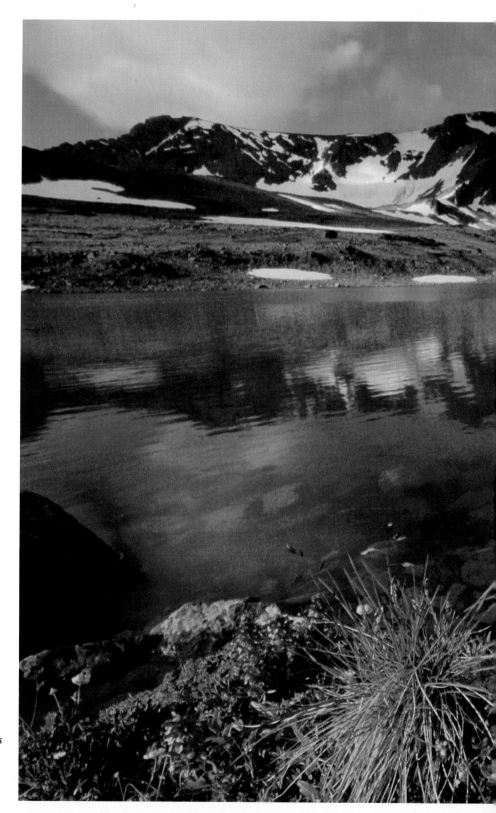

The south side of Tš'il?os

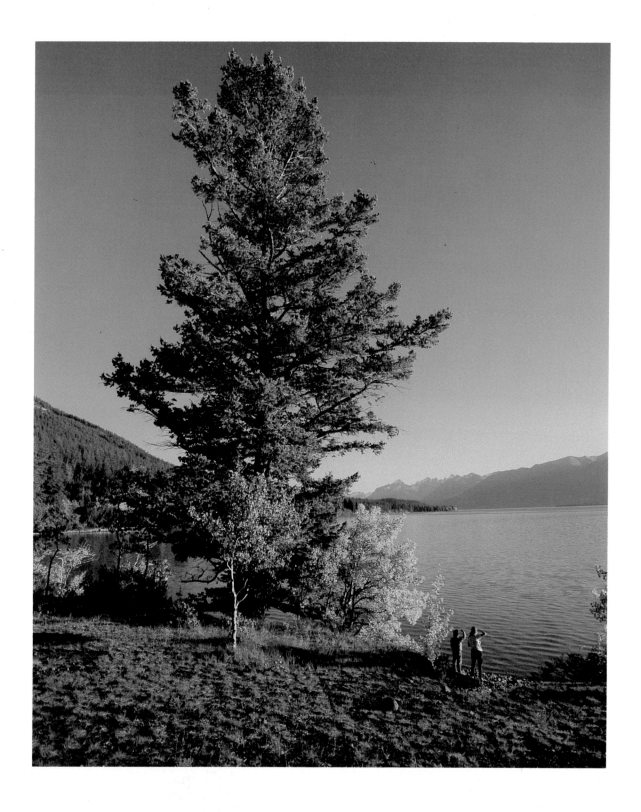

in the autumn of that year that she noticed that something was changing across the Chilcotin country.

On the road back to Nemiah from Stoney, huge clearcuts were visible from the road. The countryside was a mess, and all the band council could think to do at first was to write letters telling the logging companies to clean up the mess they were making. Those were cattle-grazing areas, and some of the cattle were getting killed, falling in the slashpiles and carnage.

In Williams Lake, all the big mills had begun to consume more timber than their government licences allowed them to cut, thanks to the government's pine beetle "salvage" policy. They were picking up timber wherever they could, and the companies knew, like Kelly Rudd said that day in front of the campfire with Henry Solomon, that a thing like that couldn't last. They were beginning to run out of wood, all of them looking for answers to the town's wood supply problems.

There was one option the government's forest planners had yet to pursue. That option could be found on a chart in the Williams Lake forest ministry offices called a TSA map.

The old TSA map shows fourteen supply blocks over a vast chunk of British Columbia's central interior around Williams Lake. The area's annual allowable cut was calculated from the eleven supply blocks within reach of the mills' feller-bunchers. The three remaining supply blocks were within the trapline of the remote Xeni gwet'in trapping area, and they remained, in the words of R.J. Reeves, district manager down at the Alexis Creek forest service office, "in the bank."

The whole idea of an annual allowable cut is to ensure a sustained harvest of the forests, but that had gone by the boards back in 1985 when the pines started turning red, and the new chart in the Williams Lake forest ministry offices showed the three Xeni gwet'in supply blocks calculated into the TSA's cut. The trees were to be withdrawn from "the bank," no longer left to stand. It was an obvious solution to the logging companies' problems.

By Annie's reckoning, if the government could get away with cutting down the Nemiah forests, the people would inevitably lose their culture, their language, their identities, the values they stand for, everything. Imagine a tree, Annie used to say. Imagine what happens when you pull a tree out by its roots.

Chilko Lake

But the one thing that had changed since the days of the Chilcotin War, Annie reckoned, was that the outside world wasn't all fury and smallpox and hostile, mercenary armies. There were alliances that might be made. There were friends and enemies alike out there.

B.C.'s growing environmental movement, which had allied itself with Indians in the Queen Charlotte Islands, on Vancouver Island's west coast, at the Stein Valley and other battlefields in the province's ongoing logging-versus-wilderness war, wanted the Nemiah people to win, too. The Xeni gwet'in territories represented the last untouched wilderness of any magnitude within the Chilcotin country, and there was no end of people who would want it left that way.

There was a group called the Niut Wilderness Society, a small group of volunteers who had put in hundreds of hours of their time, working with meagre resources and nickel-and-dime contributions from Vancouver hiker-supply stores to try to convince the government to designate the Niut Range a government-protected wilderness area. The Niut is a pristine alpine territory to the west of Tatlayoko Lake that few white people have ever seen even from a distance. There was the Federation of Mountain Clubs of B.C., a coalition that included everything from rockclimbers to birdwatchers to backpackers, which had lobbied year after year for protection for the Chilcotin country. They engaged the government in studies and consultation processes and integrated resource management plans, but they were getting nowhere with Victoria.

There was the Southern Chilcotin Mountains Wilderness Society, which took up a decades-old campaign for some kind of long-term protection for the region the Chilcotins knew as the Snow Mountains, on their southern frontiers. And even the provincial government's own parks department had hoped to ensure the preservation of the Chilko Lake country with a proposal of its own for a provincial park in the area, an idea first suggested by the Vancouver Natural History Society in 1937.

Early on in the Nemiah band's efforts to keep the logging companies at bay, the band council itself tried to draw out the government on the potential for wilderness designation as a defensive measure, but what they got from the government's district forest manager was an unusually frank letter that

left little hope for that particular idea. R.J. Reeves sat at his typewriter in the
Alexis Creek forest service office and dashed off a letter explaining that the
Nemiah country did not fit the government's own definition of wilderness as
an "uninhabited region" because the Nemiah Indians were still there.

After Reeves' response, the band council happened to raise the question
at a meeting in Williams Lake with Jack Woodward, a Victoria lawyer who'd
handled Aboriginal rights cases in the past. The meeting was supposed to be
about reserve acreage, but the talk turned to a company that wanted to start
up a helicopter-skiing business that the Nemiah people worried would scare
away all the game. And there were questions about what they could do to
stop the B.C. government from going any further with its studies of a possible
hydroelectric dam on the Homathko River. But the biggest concern was the
pace of the clearcuts making their way towards Nemiah.

The meeting ended with a plan. If the band could convince the courts that
Nemiah people have an Aboriginal right to trap, they just might be able to
prevail against clearcut logging and other activities that threatened their
trapline. So they agreed on a court case based on their trapping rights.

In Canada, the 1982 Constitution Act recognizes and affirms Aboriginal
rights, but because of squabbling among the nervous premiers after the
British North America Act was patriated, the Aboriginal rights clause remained an empty box for the courts to fill. In British Columbia, it was empty
indeed. Apart from a handful of colonial treaties on southern Vancouver
Island, no treaties were ever concluded with Aboriginal peoples west of the
Rocky Mountains. Since 1871, when B.C. joined Canada as a province, the
government in Victoria had denied the existence of Aboriginal title and
Aboriginal rights and behaved generally as though there was no obligation
to deal with Indians at all.

But most judges tended to view things a little differently. Aboriginal rights
cases were coming before the courts by the barrel load, and the Indians were
starting to win them in a big way. The idea Woodward had was that the
Nemiah people should be able to demonstrate without much problem that
they were Indians, that they were trappers, and that clearcut logging would
interfere with trapping.

On March 8, 1991, B.C.'s Indians suffered a major setback in the decision

*Carrier Lumber's operation
at Anahim Lake*

by B.C. Chief Justice Allan McEachern, who found in the Gitksan-Wet'suwet'en case that Indians in B.C. had no Aboriginal rights at all. The decision was on its way to the Supreme Court of Canada, and Woodward remained hopeful that he could wrest from the courts a finding that the Xeni gwet'in could use to stop clearcutting in the trapline area, a vast section of their traditional territory that Marvin Baptiste, when he was chief, had rolled into a single, band-owned trapline in the late 1970s.

Another ally in Nemiah's corner was the Western Canada Wilderness Committee, B.C.'s pre-eminent environmental lobby. The group had cut its teeth during the Meares campaign and the fight for South Moresby. They were constantly in battle with B.C.'s big forest companies, and they liked working with Indians. WCWC director Paul George visited the Nemiah Valley and everybody talked it over.

Backing a trapping rights case was a hard sell to make to WCWC's directors. Many of them had been active in the campaigns against leg-hold traps or just had a hard time with the whole idea of teaming up with trappers. But the directors talked it out, the WCWC joined up, and the Xeni gwet'in had the resources to stake its place with the Nemiah Declaration.

The Declaration asserts that there will be no clearcuts in the traditional territories. There will be no mining, no commercial roads and no dams. The territory will remain in Indian control, and the Indians are willing to share their country with the outside world, but on their own terms.

But there were other players at work, with other plans for the Nemiah country. By the autumn of 1990, before the snows fell, Carrier Lumber already had two grapple yarders, a de-limber and a Caterpillar tractor on the northwest corner of the trapline area. By the time the first snowfall covered the valley, there was a logging chart on the tables of P & T Mills, which had been taken over by the New Zealand forest giant Fletcher Challenge. On the chart, Eugene William' cabin and the meadows around Captain George Town were dead in the centre of six cutblocks planned for the Elkin Creek watershed. The lawyers were talking. It was just a question of when the loggers would move in, and what the Nemiah people could do to stop them.

*   *   *

The snows had come fast and heavy. They covered Tŝ'ilʔos in his winter blanket and left the road to Stoney closed for three days. Old Jack Elkins got snowed in with Willard and a couple extra hands on a brush-fence contract Elkins had taken on up the Taseko River, and it had taken him two days on the back of a work horse to make it to the Davidson Bridge, flag down a passing pickup, hitch a ride to Lee's Corner and get back up to camp with a skidder to clear a path for his truck.

So there was a good fall of snow, but so far, after two weeks of waiting, checking every couple of days and checking some more, Benny William had taken only three beaver from the traps he set in the snowbound creek down by the rodeo grounds. But then, it's early winter yet. There may be more beaver in his traps by now. Besides, it's only a couple of weeks before his lynx traps go out.

"Pretty deep in places," Benny said. It was a heck of a snowfall, and on the trail through the bush the moose tracks and the coyote tracks, even the squirrel tracks, were fresh and clear. Their trails crisscrossed the path ahead of us.

After a brisk walk of about a mile into the trees, we headed into a thicket by the rodeo grounds where a huge beaver house sat astride a snake fence.

"They'll use a stick to trigger a trap," Benny said. "They're pretty smart."

The point is to outsmart them, and they're smart enough to flood out the rodeo grounds entirely if they're left to their own devices. So Benny had set three conibear traps, the type that drowns them quickly, in the runways they'd cleared for themselves in the creek ice. We checked one, then another, then the third. We reset the third, and Benny poked a hole or two at the lip of their dam. The idea is that they'll head out to investigate the problem when they notice water spilling over the dam, swim through their runways and maybe even get caught in one of Benny's traps.

"Think I might have to work myself further down, or maybe up the creek," Benny said. "But I wanted to get these first, because if I don't, they'll flood the place out."

Nothing here today, Benny said. He'd check later and if he was really lucky he'd find a beaver or two to bring home with him. He worries about this year's price list for furs, and he says he can't figure out those people who call themselves environmentalists who fight so hard against trapping. The way he sees it, he said, trapping was what the Nemiah people had always done, and it sure beat logging everything out.

Benny was counting on the trapping rights case to win, because if it didn't, the war would go on and there was no telling where it might lead. Maybe it would mean roadblocks. Maybe a lot of things.

"You look at Tŝ'ilʔos," he said, about the mountain that used to be a man. "He'll get back at you somehow. Maybe today, maybe tomorrow, but sometime. You'll be out there without a tent, maybe. But he'll get back at you, somehow."

"That's the other part of it," he said, "and that's if we lost, after having fought so long. People would give up, I think.

"Most of our traditional hunting area on the other side of the river's already been logged off. Seymour Draw, those meadows in there. And once we let them across the bridge, they're not going to stop there. They'll take every patch there is. That's why I think it's really important that we don't let them cross the bridge."

But they're getting close. Last year, the Davidson Bridge was upgraded, and the only consolation is that the bridge still probably couldn't handle much heavy logging traffic, Benny figures.

"I'd like to see things left as it is," Benny says. "I don't want it looking like a clearcut. It's so beautiful now."

It's hard to argue with that on our way back to Benny's house, a short walk through the trees from the band office, where out back, the pelts of two beaver were stretching in the cold air.

The big one was four feet in length, and stretched, with its tail, it makes almost six feet of beaver. It's hard work, trapping, skinning and stretching a pelt, and that big one won't likely bring him more than $60, with a lot less for the small one.

That night, after dinner, Annie agreed that sometimes it's tough to make a living out of the Chilcotin bush. Sure, she said. It's hard getting by out here.

But it's worth it, she's quick to add. And it's been worth the hard times as chief, too, although she asked herself why she's bothered, and more than once.

"So why?" she asked herself, and sat on the couch and thought about it awhile.

*Edmond Lulua
hauling moosemeat
out of the bush*

A beehive burner

"I couldn't tell you why."

Across the room, her husband, Walter Lulua, sat in his chair and smiled.

"Deep in your heart, you know," he said.

Annie laughed.

"I don't really know. I thought maybe with the education I had behind me, it would be no problem. I didn't know you had to be a lawyer, a teacher, a good listener. But I've got to switch from being a leader of our people, a parent and myself. It's hard. One person told me when something happened at the school, 'You're not talking as a parent. You're talking as a chief.' I keep asking myself, 'how do you separate these things?' You can't. I haven't, anyway. Maybe you can, I don't know. But not in my culture, anyway."

If being a chief has been hard, being a mother hasn't been any easier.

Annie and Walter have raised five of their six children. There's Florence, eighteen, Lynda, thirteen, ten-year-old Wesley, who prefers to be known as Mr. Wesley, seven-year-old Erikk and the baby, Shelton, who's just a year old. Nine-year-old Melissa was given over to another Chilcotin family who had asked Annie for a child before Melissa was born.

Those were the ones that lived. Two were stillborn, one was lost to crib death, and another died of pneumonia.

Annie's 35, and Walter is 40. At least he thinks he is, but he's not sure.

"He was wild," Annie says about Walter, and she's only partly kidding, because Walter grew up in the mountains around Nemiah, living off the land with his family, the old way.

"Nobody ever saw him," Annie says. "You'd hear about him, but you never saw him.

"I tamed him," she says.

Walter sat quietly and smiled. He wasn't arguing. The snow was falling outside, and Annie talked about what the fight over the logging was really all about.

"This is about our culture, our way of life," Annie said.

"You see in other Chilcotin reserves, where it's clearcut all around them. There's nothing for them to do but go to Williams Lake, Alexis Creek, Lee's Corner. They drink and they drink, they know it's killing them, but there's

THE RAVEN COPYING MAN

As told by William Setah

One day the Raven got very hungry. He asked the people staying not very far from his place if they could give him something to eat because he was starving. The person staying there, his name was Yinaxun. Yinaxun's wife went walking, carrying a can. She said she was going to pick some berries. She didn't take very long, then she came back with a can full of berries. She really filled the can full of berries in just a little while. She brought the berries back in the house and gave it to the Raven. The Raven was delighted. He said, "I will bring it back home with me. When I am finished, I will bring the can back."

When the Raven arrived home, he brought the can back outside and said, "I want this can to be full of berries." Then the can only had a few dry berries in it. The Raven just ate it anyway. He thought he could do that again and get some more. He danced around a bit first, then he said, "I want this can to be full of bad things." It happened, too. Everything that was bad filled the can. Yinaxun's wife, the one that gave the berries to the Raven, got really mad and hit the Raven around. She washed the can out really good and went back to the house.

Once again, the Raven got very hungry, so he went to Nusilxatsi's home and asked for some food. Nusilxatsi picked up a plate and some rocks. He started hitting the Raven's feet with small rocks, and some fish eggs came falling out. That plate Nusilxatsi had filled quite a bit. The Raven ate really lots, then he turned to Nusilxatsi and said, "I will bring the other half I didn't eat back to my place. When I finish with it you can come and pick it up."

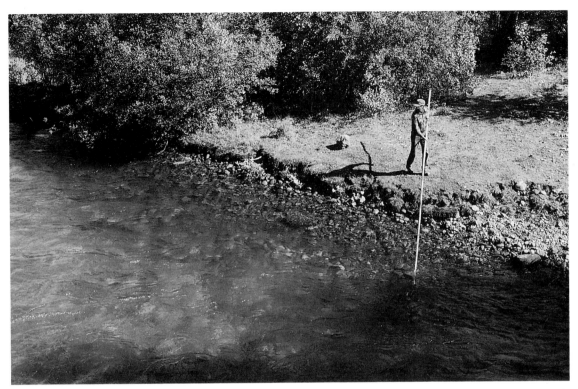

Ubill Lulua gaffing salmon

When Nusilxatsi got to the Raven's place, the Raven thought he would do it again so he started hitting his feet with rocks. Only one fish egg fell out. The Raven got really mad, then started hitting his feet with rocks. The rocks were almost gone. No fish eggs came out.

Nusilxatsi just picked up his plate and went back home.

nothing for them to do. We're lucky. We're so lucky, because that hasn't happened here."

As always, Walter backs her up. If there's one thing they've never disagreed on, it was Annie's decision to serve as chief. In Chilcotin country, it's got so that the men do the wage work when there's wage work to be done and women are more or less expected to sit up and pay attention. But like a lot of things in Chilcotin country, those kinds of changes haven't quite made it to Nemiah.

By the spring of 1991, the chief's job was handed over to Roger William. And Roger's just as committed to holding the line as Annie and Benny.

It's just something that has to be done. It isn't easy, with 24 head of cattle that Roger and Gene Cooper and Roger's mother Eileen have to take care of. But there's Colton to think about, Roger says. Colton is Roger's little boy.

The Nemiah Valley should be there for Colton when he gets older, Roger says.

"I'd like to tell him," Roger said. "I'd like to show him."

Which, he said, is probably the kind of thing the people were thinking back in the days of the Chilcotin War.

"I think our people, the Chilcotin, they were scared of losing all this land," he said. "I mean, look at us now. We still have our language, a lot of our beliefs, we still have a lot of religion. I think that's the reason why, the Chilcotin War is why we're here today. The way we think, the way we talk and the way we live. I think if they just came in and out and people did nothing, it would be really something else. But we won.

"If you clearcut here, it would be really hard for us to keep the way we live, even to keep our language, even for our ladies to make moccasins and that, because it's going to be hard to get the deer or moose. And I think we want to be self-sufficient. I'm not talking land claims, because the land's ours anyway. And the government's going to say, 'You guys don't even know your language, you don't even know the way you live, you don't even know how you govern yourselves.' And we know that now. If you get rid of the trees, you're slowly going to lose it."

So far, Roger William hasn't lost much of anything.

Then again, he didn't win the mountain race at last year's Nemiah Valley

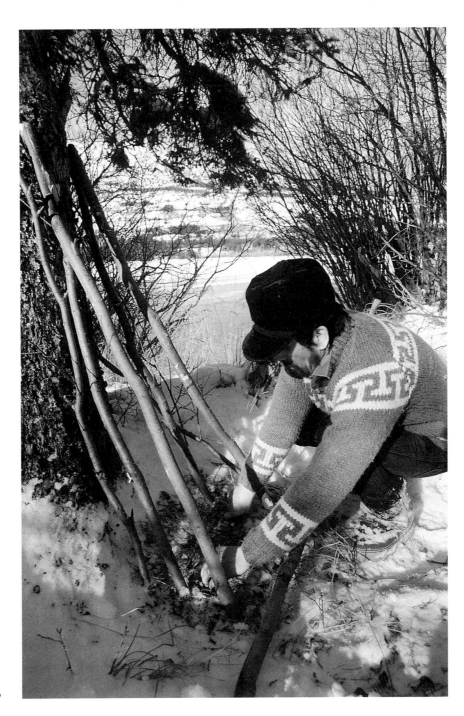

Boysie William setting trap

Rodeo. His horse got scared of the crowd and spooked in the last stretch. Harry Setah was leading all the way in that race. David Setah was leading the day before, but David Setah's horse fell in the creek. Roger was third behind him, Harry was second, but Harry's horse got scared. Roger was on his mother's horse. Roger won that day.

The upshot was that Roger placed second, overall. But he has won four times, all told, so he really can't complain.

Besides, there's Tŝ'ilʔos to think about.

"You don't point at it or anything like that," Roger said. "He'll get you. Maybe next year, maybe five years away, maybe tomorrow, but it'll get you."

And Tŝ'ilʔos has done what he can to help. Annie and Walter and Roger swear they're certain of it, no matter how it might sound to people from outside the valley. There was that time when Annie and Walter went to Ashcroft to meet with an assembly of Shuswap, Lillooet and Thompson chiefs. Annie forgot to bring a copy of the Nemiah Declaration, so Walter went out to see if they had one in the truck, and there was a pile of them there that Walter says he certainly didn't bring and Annie says she didn't bring, either. They both say it must have been Tŝ'ilʔos.

ʔEniyud is a real person, too. She is the woman, and she is said to be the keeper of strange animals, like some sort of manta ray in Eagle Lake that has been known to walk on land and leave tracks that people have come across when they're out looking for cattle. But it is Tŝ'ilʔos that guards the Xeni gwet'in, as Annie is sure he did when they were touring the prairies with the Nemiah Declaration, trying to raise support for their trapping rights case, when a tornado hit Calgary and the gale-force winds washed out roads everywhere but left a path for them wherever they went.

"Seems like he made a way for us and left everybody else on the other side," Annie said. "Seems like he was with us all the time."

"He is a real person," Annie said confidently. "He'll take care of us."

Susie Setah with her baby,
Nicole

A F T E R W O R D

Statement from the Nemiah Valley Indian Band

We are one of six Indian bands of the Chilcotin Nation. There are the Alexandria Indian Band, the Toosey Indian Band, the Anaham Indian Band, the Stone Indian Band, and the Alexis Creek (Redstone) Indian Band. Then there is the Nemiah Valley Indian Band.

We are the only Chilcotin band that big industry has not touched. We hear and see the negative effects of development from the other Chilcotin bands. That is why we are protecting our heritage. That is why we issued the Nemiah Declaration on August 23, 1989, and why we sought and won an injunction against logging companies on October 11, 1991.

Since July, 1991, we have been working together with the B.C. Parks and the Ministry of Mines on the Chilko Lake Park Proposal Study Team. As a result of a dispute regarding the Henry's Crossing Bridge, in May, 1992, we are now working on a Brittany Forest Management Plan for all of the Territory covered by our Declaration.

This book will give you some idea about our heritage and our goals. We, the Xeni gwet'in people of Nemiah, are only saying what our elders have always said. "If you take care of and respect the land you live on, the land will take care of you." That is why we made our Declaration — to protect the land.

The face of Tŝ'ilʔos is shown on our Declaration. He looks over us. Our elders have passed this down to us, as it has been passed down to them by their elders, since time began. We believe that Tŝ'ilʔos will protect us and the land we live on. For this reason, we are taking action today for our next generations, and for our forefathers before us.

We hope you enjoyed this book. Thank you for your time.

From the Great Spirits
and the Xeni gwet'in
(People of Nemiah Valley)
August 4, 1992

SOURCES

Alexander, Diane. "Report on the Potato Mountain Archeological Project."
Unpublished report prepared for the Social Sciences and Humanities Research
Council of Canada, the Heritage Conservation Branch of British Columbia, and
the Nemiah Valley Indian Band Council, May 1987.

Alexander, Diane, Robert Tyhurst, Linda Burnard-Hogarth, and R.G. Matson. "A
Preliminary Ethnoarchaeological Investigation of the Potato Mountain Range
and Eagle Lake Area." Unpublished report prepared for the Heritage
Conservation Branch of British Columbia, Canadian Ethnic Studies Program,
and the Nemiah Valley Indian Band Council, May 1985.

Brown, C. Lundin. *Klatsassan, and Other Reminiscences of Missionary Life in British
Columbia*. London: Society for Promoting Christian Knowledge, 1873.

Carrier Lumber Ltd. "Management and Working Plan for the period January 1,
1984 to December 31, 1993, Forest Licence A20022." October 1984.

Farrand, Livingston. *Traditions of the Chilcotin Indians*. New York: AMS Press, 1990
(reprint, New York: American Museum of Natural History, 1900).

Glavin, Terry. Series on relations between Chilcotin people and justice system,
Vancouver *Sun*, February-April 1989.

Gray, Robert W. "The Mountain Pine Beetle." Unpublished paper, Vancouver,
1989[?].

Hatler, Dave. "Presentation to Northern Silviculture Committee winter meeting."
Northern Interior Trappers Association, March 20, 1989.

Hewlett, Edward Sleigh. "The Chilcotin Uprising: A Study of Indian-White
Relations in Nineteenth Century British Columbia." MA thesis, Department of
History, Vancouver: University of British Columbia, March 1972.

Hewlett, Edward Sleigh. "The Chilcotin Uprising of 1864." *B.C. Studies* 19, Autumn
1973.

Howay, F.W. "The Bute Inlet Massacre and the Chilcotin War," in *British Columbia: From Earliest Times to the Present*, Vol. 2. Vancouver: S.J. Clarke, 1914, pp. 177-201.

Kimmins, J.P. "Report to the South Chilcotin Mountains Wilderness Society Concerning Potential Boundaries for a South Chilcotin Mountain Wilderness Park." Unpublished paper, Vancouver, 1985.

Lane, Robert Brockstedt. "Cultural Relations of the Chilcotin Indians of West Central British Columbia." PhD thesis, Department of Philosophy, Seattle: University of Washington, 1953.

Magne, Martin. "Taseko Lakes Prehistory Project: Report On A Preliminary Survey." Unpublished paper, prepared for the British Columbia Heritage Trust and the Nemiah Valley Indian Band Council, January 1984.

Magne, Martin, and R.G. Matson. "Athapaskan and Earlier Archaeology at Big Eagle Lake, British Columbia." Unpublished paper, Vancouver: University of British Columbia Archeology Laboratory, August 1984.

Morice, Adrian Gabriel. *History of the Northern Interior of British Columbia, Formerly New Caledonia. History of British Columbia.* Toronto: William Briggs, 1904.

Mueller, F.M., J.S. Hart, and A.C. Mayall. "Proposal For a Wilderness Area in the Niut Range." Niut Wilderness Society, September 1989.

Nalbach, James T. "Potential Effects of Forest Industrial Operations on Other Resource Use Options in the West Chilcotin Area." Report prepared for the Chilcotin Survival Coalition, May 1986.

Nyland, Edo. "Draft Report: Forestry." Unpublished paper prepared for the Nemiah Valley Indian Band Council, no date.

Parfitt, Ben. Various articles on forest industry in Chilcotin, Vancouver *Sun*, 1988- .

Reeves, R.J., B.C. Forests Ministry, Alexis Creek. Miscellaneous correspondence to Nemiah Valley Indian Band, 1987-1989.

Rothenburger, Mel. *The Chilcotin War.* Langley, B.C.: Mr. Paperback, 1978.

Southern Chilcotin Mountains Wilderness Society. "The South Chilcotin Mountains: Recommendations for Recreation Area. Draft Presentation to Environment and Land Use Committee, January 5, 1990." Unpublished paper, Gold Bridge, B.C.: 1990.

Thomas, Father François Marie. "Indian Wars of the Cariboo." *Cariboo and Northern B.C. Digest*, Winter 1946.

Ts'ilhqot'in Tribal Council, Cariboo Tribal Council, Chilcotin-Ulkatcho-Kluskus Tribal Council. "Submission to the B.C. Ministry of Forests re: Proposed Pulpwood Area No. 19 (Chilcotin) and the Proposed Agreement No. 19 and Two Pending Applications." January 18, 1990.

Tyhurst, Robert. "The Chilcotin: An Ethnographic History (Revised Draft)." Unpublished paper, July 1984.